SCOTTISH RAILWAYS

IN THE 1960s

Alves was the junction station for the Burghead branch, seen with HR No. 103 on 21 April 1962.

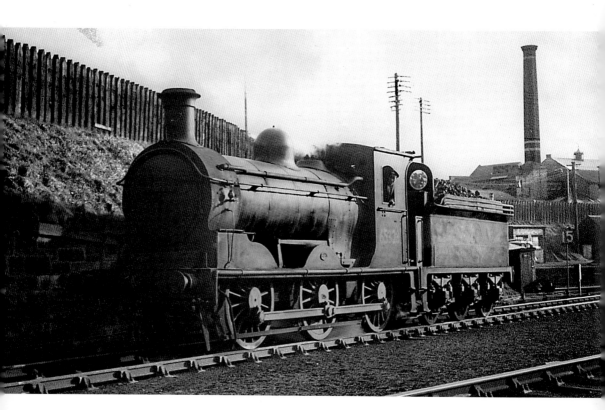

'J36' No. 65323 stands at Alloa on 13 April 1963.

SCOTTISH RAILWAYS

IN THE 1960s

MICHAEL CLEMENS

FONTHILL

A 'Jubilee' storms through Beattock during Easter 1962.

Fonthill Media Language Policy

Fonthill Media publishes in the international English language market. One language edition is published worldwide. As there are minor differences in spelling and presentation, especially with regard to American English and British English, a policy is necessary to define which form of English to use. The Fonthill Policy is to use the form of English native to the author. Michael Clemens was born and educated in Worcestershire, England; therefore, British English has been adopted in this publication.

Fonthill Media Limited
Fonthill Media LLC
www.fonthillmedia.com
office@fonthillmedia.com

First published in the United Kingdom and the United States of America 2019

British Library Cataloguing in Publication Data:
A catalogue record for this book is available from the British Library

Copyright © Michael Clemens 2019

ISBN 978-1-78155-761-7

Typeset in 10.5pt on 13pt Sabon
Printed and bound in England

Introduction

By the middle of the 1950s, it had become obvious to my father (C. N. 'Jim' Clemens, 1922–1987) that the railways of Britain were undergoing a period of tremendous change after having remained fairly static for some decades. In particular, many branch lines and some secondary routes were being closed down, together with the withdrawal of the steam locomotives that had worked over them. I am sure that when he started recording this fast-disappearing scene in the 1950s, he did not realise just what a massive undertaking it would become. The film archive he created—both ciné and still—covered not just our Worcestershire locality but from Cornwall to the north of Scotland. As long as it did not conflict with school, I was generally with my father on his railway travels, and assisted more and more as the years went by. Yet let there be no doubt, the credit for the massive collection that was built up over the years lies with my father.

This is my eleventh photo-book about British railways in the late 1950s and 1960s, the seventh for Fonthill Media, and my second covering purely Scotland. For those who have read my earlier books, this latest one—*Scottish Railways in the 1960s*—follows a similar format. The uniqueness of this book again lies in its photographs—a mixture of colour plus black and white, virtually all of which have never been published before. They were taken by me, my father, or our friend Alan Maund (1930–1983). In the main, the time period covered is from the late 1950s through to the mid-1960s. The BR system dominates, although a few industrial sites are also visited, where steam could still be sought out well into the 1970s. Steam is the main motive power throughout, but an exception is a journey along the line from Inverness to Thurso in July 1963, by which time this route was entirely diesel operated. This book will appeal to railway enthusiasts, modellers, and those interested in local history.

The 'Scottish Rambler No. 2' rail tour waits at Barrhill on 15 April 1963; a number of relevant tickets are also included throughout this book, as here.

Amazingly for the era, we did make day return trips from Worcestershire to Scotland in both 1963 ('Duchess Commemorative' rail tour) and 1964 ('Scottish Lowlander' rail tour), but most of our visits would be for just under one week. Our Easter visits beginning in 1962 would correspond with the 'Scottish Rambler' tours that we both filmed and travelled on. Very often, we would stop with my father's eldest first cousin and family at 36 Old Coach Road, East Kilbride; her husband had set up the Philips factory at Hamilton in the years after the Second World War. Sometimes, we would travel from home by road (which always seemed an interminably long journey), sometimes by rail, and once by air (November 1965).

In very broad terms, *Scottish Railways in the 1960s* makes a clockwise journey around Scotland, beginning at Beattock before moving to Dumfries. Here for the first time, we encounter one of the four pre-Grouping locomotives restored to working order in Scotland during the late 1950s and often used on enthusiasts' specials around the country. From Dumfries, a trip is made over the 'Port Road' to Stranraer via Castle Douglas, New Galloway, and the Whithorn branch; the latter was with haulage by one of the last Caledonian Railway 'Jumbos' designed some eighty years previously.

The National Coal Board (NCB) system at Waterside (Ayrshire) is visited in 1978 before coverage some twenty years earlier of the former Glasgow and South Western Railway's (G&SWR) largely goods-only lines east of Ayr at Tarbolton, Drongan, Skares, Lugar, and Muirkirk. We continue east of Muirkirk on the old Caledonian Railway (CR) route via Inches, Douglas West, and Happendon to

Shunting at Blair Atholl during July 1963. (*Alan Maund*)

The terminus at Brechin lost its passenger service in 1952; ten years later, D8028 pays a visit.

the railway centre of Carstairs. More 1959 film follows along another one-time CR line—that from Coalburn via Lesmahagow, Blackwood, and Stonehouse to Larkhall. Not far from our East Kilbride base was another location visited in 1959: the semi-derelict station at High Blantyre that would close entirely in 1960.

More coverage follows at Glasgow, Paisley, and Greenock before moving to another industrial location that was the final place in Scotland where steam locomotives were used commercially: the Sentinel-type engines at R. B. Tennent's foundry, Whifflet, Coatbridge. The final place to work conventional steam locomotives in Scotland is also seen at Bedlay Colliery, plus also Glenboig and Lennoxtown on the BR system. How many of us fondly recall the 1960s TV classic of *Dr. Finlay's Casebook*? The fictional town of Tannochbrae was supposedly part-based on the next place we visit of Callander; perhaps there might even be time to visit Arden House for a cup of tea with Janet. We head westwards after Callander to Killin Junction, seen during a 1963 snowstorm, before a trip along the branch to Killin and Loch Tay, then Dalmally and Ballachulish.

One of the most scenic lines in Britain is the West Highland Railway that stretches from the banks of the Clyde to Fort William and Mallaig. The line struck

Parts of the 1960s TV classic *Dr. Finlay's Casebook* were filmed here at Callander; No. 42168 simmers away in July 1963. (*Alan Maund*)

Between Callander and Strathyre during 1963. (*Alan Maund*)

Approaching Oykel Viaduct between Culrain and Invershin in July 1963; it marks the border between the historic counties of Ross-shire and Sutherland. (*Alan Maund*)

north and included about 30 miles of barren and roadless country that was some of the most desolate in Europe. Coverage along this route includes the isolated crossing place of Gorton, then Rannoch, Fort William, Glenfinnan Viaduct, and Arisaig. In July 1963, our friend, the late Alan Maund, visited what is often called the 'Far North Line'. This begins at Inverness where his wife, Wendy, is seen posing by the side of 'The Orcadian' awaiting departure, and then northwards through Lairg, Golspie, Dunrobin, Helmsdale, Kildonan, and Kinbrace before time is spent exploring the most northerly junction on BR (Georgemas Junction) and finally terminating at Thurso.

Our journey east from Inverness is made on the Easter 1962 'Scottish Rambler', the first of six successive Easter 'Rambles' organised by the Branch Line Society

Above: An undated view of No. 60011 *Empire of India* standing at the east end of Edinburgh Waverley. (*Alan Maund*)

Opposite above: The most northerly junction on the BR system; Georgemas Junction is seen in the summer of 1963. (*Alan Maund*)

Opposite below: The gradient post in the foreground indicates No. 61342 has just reached the top of the 1 in 72 after leaving Girvan for Ayr on 10 April 1966; its exertions that day can be freely listened to via the author's website, michaelclemensrailways.co.uk.

and others. It gave the opportunity to visit rare and closed branch lines and proved a great success. According to the 1962 tour report, 'nearly 1,000 miles were covered and well over 100 enthusiasts from as far afield as Plymouth and Thurso took part', the five-coach train including a buffet car. The visit we will make to Burghead Harbour is described in glowing terms: 'With the colourful loco perched on the seawall above the sparkling waves and a blue sky, an even bluer sea and the fishing boats bobbing about in the harbour ... a colourful highlight of the tour'. Visits are also made to Gollanfield, Elgin, Insch, and Turriff. Included on the next day (Easter Sunday) were Brechin, Edzell, Montrose, Inverbervie, and the delightful Carmyllie branch. Easter Monday included Perth, Bankfoot, and Forfar.

Above: 'A4' No. 60006 *Sir Ralph Wedgewood* prepares to depart Gleneagles for Glasgow on 4 June 1965. (*Alan Maund*)

Opposite above: The 'Jacobite' rail tour locomotives stand at the isolated and lonely crossing place of Gorton (Rannoch Moor) on 1 June 1963.

Opposite below: On Good Friday 1963, CR No. 123 stands amongst fresh snow at Killin Junction.

Main line action follows at Gleneagles with 'A4' No. 60006 in 1965 and then visits to Auchtermuchty, the strangely named Rumbling Bridge, Alloa, Alva, Dunfermline, and North Queensferry before crossing to the south bank of the Forth. Film then follows at Bathgate, St Margarets shed (Edinburgh), Niddrie West Junction, Duns, and Wooler (the only place visited in the main body of this book not in Scotland), to conclude at Hawick and the Waverley Route.

For those interested in further coverage of the railways of Scotland, I have released three videos using the ciné film we took: Scotland Revisited Parts I, II, and III. Also, a number of locomotive tape recordings we made are freely available (mostly at broadcast standard) in the Sound Bites section of my website, as are all the tickets, plus thousands of pages of printed railway memorabilia, including working timetables. For further details, visit michaelclemensrailways.co.uk for a railway enthusiast's delight.

Above: 'Jubilee' No. 45675 *Hardy* passes Lugton in the summer of 1958.

Opposite above: The tiny locomotive depot at Loch Tay is in the background on a snowy 12 April 1963.

Opposite below: On 10 April 1966, 'B1' No. 61342 runs around its train at Muirkirk.

I would like to thank in no particular order various societies and individuals who have freely given me their help in compiling this book: Monmouthshire Railway Society; Severn Valley Railway Association (Stourbridge Branch); South Devon Railway Club; Chipping Norton Railway Club; Jeff Sedgley; Bruce McCartney; Glasgow and South Western Railway Association (in particular Stuart Rankin); and the Caledonian Railway Association.

Michael Clemens,
Pershore
Worcestershire,
December 2018

The north end of Perth Station on 23 April 1962 as No. 54465 catches the morning sun.

Yet it is the evening sun at Stranraer Town on 15 April 1963 with HR No. 103 and GNSR No. 49 *Gordon Highlander*.

The last place to operate steam locomotives commercially in Scotland was R. B. Tennent's foundry at Whifflet, Coatbridge. Sentinel-type locomotive *Denis* is at work during May 1978.

The NCB Waterside system in Ayrshire during May 1978; locally built No. 24 is hard at work.

We travelled from Crewe to Edingurgh and back in a day on the 'Duchess Commemorative' rail tour; No. 46251 *City of Nottingham* awaits departure from Edinburgh Princes Street on 5 October 1963.

SCOTTISH
RAILWAYS
IN THE 1960s

Descending from Drumochter summit (1,484 feet) in the summer of 1963. (*Alan Maund*)

Scottish Railways in the 1960s begins its journey around the country at Beattock on 2 June 1965 as 'Britannia' No. 70001 *Lord Hurcomb* (first chairman of the British Transport Commission) arrives from the south.

By 1844, a rail network in England connected Exeter in the south-west all the way to Tyneside in the north-east. In Scotland, Glasgow had been connected to Edinburgh since 1842, plus there were numerous other railways already open around this time, albeit not all built to today's standard-gauge. What did not exist was a rail link between England and Scotland. The broad idea of a trunk line between Lancashire and Glasgow came from the Grand Junction Railway, whose head engineering office was to be established at Crewe. Before the GJR was even open for traffic, they sent civil engineer Joseph Locke to make preliminary surveys of a route to not only Glasgow, but also Edinburgh. It became a battle between two routes— Annandale and via Beattock, or Nithsdale and via Dumfries and Kilmarnock. The Government of the day became involved as it was felt traffic would support just a single-trunk rail link, and a commission was set up in 1839. Yet by 1841, when the commission's reports were issued, ideas had changed; signs pointed to the need for two or possibly even more routes within a few years. (*Alan Maund*)

Another photograph taken by our friend the late Alan Maund at Beattock on 2 June 1965; D338, an English Electric Type 4 (the later Class 40), races past non-stop with service 1M37, believed to be the 12.20 p.m. through train from Perth to London Euston. Beattock station was still open at the time and would not close until the beginning of 1972; there is now just the one intermediate station still open along the 73.5 miles from Carstairs to Carlisle: Lockerbie. If there was one of the diesel 'pilot scheme' designs that could be expected to be a guaranteed success, this was it. It was a direct development of the pioneer LMS and SR designs built in 1947 and 1950 respectively. First deliveries entered service in 1958 on Great Eastern services to Norwich, plus also the East Coast Main Line where, for a while, they were the diesel equivalent of steam's Gresley Pacifics. Further orders were placed, and by September 1962, when the final class member was constructed, there were 200 in service. Locomotive designer E. S. Cox published casualty figures relating to English Electric diesels for 1965: Class 20—116,000 miles per casualty; Class 37—18,000 miles; and Class 40—10,000 miles, (it was said of the Class 08 shunters that casualties and defects were almost unknown). The heyday of the class was probably the early 1960s, when they worked the principle expresses along the West Coast Main Line. However, they were relatively low powered (2,000 hp), rather on the heavy side (133 tons), and by the date of this photograph were being displaced on services such as these by what became the Class 47s (2,750 hp and 114 tons). In fact, that same day, Alan photographed Class 47 D1845 passing through Beattock in pristine condition and only a matter of days old. (*Alan Maund*)

Alan has left neither the date nor the locomotive number with this photograph, but there is a location—Harthope, on Beattock bank—close to where the old A74 main road passed underneath the railway towards the summit of the grade from Beattock Station, and, clearly, the locomotive is a 'Black 5'.

Joseph Locke's initial survey of the Annandale route went well until he reached a point about 3 miles to the south of what is now Beattock Summit. He found this area so steep and sustained an ascent, through so rough and bleak a landscape, that he turned back and began a survey of Nithsdale instead. His calculations had shown if the gradient to Beattock Summit was not to exceed that which he already had in mind for crossing the Shap Fells, the incline would have to start as far back as Beattock village. Nevertheless, the Annandale route via Beattock was eventually chosen, and in no small part due to pressure from the MP for Dumfriesshire, and Charles Stewart, factor of the Annandale estates. It was Stewart who said the line from the south and over Beattock could be seen as a spear that that became a trident: the left-hand prong to Glasgow, the right to Edinburgh, and straight on to Stirling, Perth, and the north. Locke settled on the Annandale route as it was the shortest, even though a consequence was the long and steep gradient to Beattock Summit. He believed shorter routes could be finished more quickly with less cost, allowing revenue to start earlier; it became known as the 'up and over' school of engineering. Royal Assent for the Annandale route was given in July 1845 and was open throughout by 1848, becoming the Caledonian Railway. Authorisation had also been obtained for the Nithsdale line, which was open by 1850. (*Alan Maund*)

There used to be a railway that connected Annandale to Nithsdale, or more precisely Lockerbie to Dumfries: the Dumfries, Lochmaben and Lockerbie Railway. While by 1850 the towns at either end had the benefits of a railway such as cheap coal, Lochmaben (population 3,100 in 1851) did not. The DL&LR was promoted independently to open up this mainly agricultural area as local farmers were looking for a cheaper source of fertiliser in addition to an outlet for their produce. Royal Assent was obtained in June 1860 and services started at the beginning of September 1863. With their eyes on the Irish traffic, the Caledonian Railway absorbed the DL&LR in July 1865, following which the CR owned, jointly owned, or had gained running rights from Lockerbie to Dumfries and all the way to Stranraer and Portpatrick. There were now two competing routes from Carlisle to Dumfries for traffic to the north of Ireland from England: the direct Glasgow and South Western Railway (G&SWR) route via Annan and the longer CR route via Lockerbie. Yet following the formation of the Portpatrick and Wigtownshire Joint Railway in 1886 (jointly owned by the Caledonian, Glasgow and South Western, London and North Western, and Midland railways), the bitter competition was diminished and the railway from Dumfries to Lockerbie became more of a local branch line. Passenger services ceased in May 1952, with complete closure coming some fourteen years later. On Sunday, 17 October 1965, this enthusiasts' special is making its way from Dumfries to Lockerbie and is filmed from the road between West and East Lanegate. The tour is hauled by restored Highland Railway No. 103, its last outing as a working locomotive before taking up residency in the Glasgow Museum of Transport.

Restored HR No. 103 is seen being serviced at Dumfries shed on 17 October 1965. It was working a Branch Line Society round trip from Glasgow to Dumfries over the G&SWR line, then back to Glasgow via Beattock (see the previous photograph). The second photograph is taken at the north end of Dumfries station on Easter Monday, 15 April 1963 and shows 'Jubilee' No 45588 *Kashmir* awaiting departure along the 'Port Road' to (eventually) Stranraer. This was the final day of the joint Stephenson Locomotive Society's (SLS) (Scottish Area) and Branch Line Society's (BLS) 'Scottish Rambler No. 2 Easter Rail Tour'; it had started on Good Friday. This tour had earlier passed over the branch from Lockerbie to Dumfries; No. 45588 was then turned at the shed before continuing westwards. Dumfries station had two main platforms with bay lines at the north end on the down side; these bays were generally used by Stranraer line services. There were separate up and down lines parallel to the main Carlisle to Glasgow tracks; this allowed a totally clear run into or from the station for Stranraer services, with the actual junction being about a quarter of a mile to the north.

The author's father visited Scotland by rail during Whitsun 1959, travelling northbound over what could be considered the obvious routing (the West Coast Main Line), but he decided to do something a bit different for the return. Presenting himself at Glasgow St Enoch station's ticket office, he asked for a single to Worcester Shrub Hill, travelling on the 'Thames-Clyde Express' via the Nithsdale route, Ais Gill Summit, Leeds, Sheffield, and then on connecting services to Birmingham and Worcester. He thought this seemingly more obscure routing would cause confusion in the ticket office—though not at all as the required single ticket was supplied with no problem; its cost was £2 19s 4d (5s 8d more expensive than travelling via Crewe, though sadly, the ticket has not survived). These two photographs are taken on this return journey on Monday, 11 May 1959, at what was Solway Junction, Annan, but now controlled by Solway GF (ground frame). The single track branching off gave connection to the line over the Solway Viaduct (closed in 1921) and latterly for goods only to Annan Shawhill Station (closed February 1955). Considering this line had been supposedly closed for over four years, it seems to be in excellent condition.

Castle Douglas, where both photographs are taken, is an important market town in Galloway and junction station for the Kirkcudbright branch. The first, at the west end of the station, shows the joint SLS/BLS Easter tour of Scotland on 15 April 1963. We saw this tour at Dumfries previously; here, at Castle Douglas, No. 45588 *Kashmir* came off the train and is now being replaced by BR Standard Class 4 2-6-4T No. 80023, which would haul the special to Kirkcudbright and back. On return from Kirkcudbright, the tour was handed back to the 'Jubilee' and headed for Stranraer. The second photograph dates from Good Friday, 16 April 1965, when the author and his father made a return journey from Dumfries to Stranraer, the route closing some two months later. By this time, the 8.07 a.m. from Dumfries ran as a combined service to Castle Douglas where the train split into portions for Kirkcudbright and Stranraer. However, the Stranraer portion offered an advertised connection off the overnight sleeper service from London that was running late. Thus, the Kirkcudbright portion on which we travelled did depart at 8.07 a.m., alighting at Castle Douglas to await the late running Stranraer portion that is seen arriving behind No. 44995.

New Galloway station, about 9 miles to the west of Castle Douglas and a passing loop on the largely single-track section onwards to Stranraer; the railway was double track from Dumfries to Castle Douglas. This is another photograph taken on Good Friday 1965 during a journey from Dumfries to Stranraer and our train in the foreground with 'Black 5' 44995 was running behind schedule; it was meant to pass the train in the background at the next loop to the west—the legendary and lonely Loch Skerrow with no road access. The eastbound train is the 8 a.m. stopping service from Stranraer to Dumfries, hauled by Class 4 tank No. 80119 (and misread in my earlier book on Scottish railways off the ciné film we took as No. 80114).

This is a very remote area, the town of New Galloway being some 5 miles distant. The author as a young lad thought it very strange the railway took this inland, sparsely populated, and steeply graded route over the Galloway Moors between Castle Douglas and Newton Stewart instead of following the coast where most people lived. The answer to this conundrum is that the railway's objective was the Irish traffic, with local business not being a prime concern. Also, land was much cheaper over the moors and this led to constructional costs of around £7,500 per mile, less than a quarter of the usual figure.

Sometimes, my father would purchase tickets just to add to his collection and these are two such examples—an LMSR motorcycle parking ticket from Creetown plus a privilege single from Gatehouse of Fleet to Creetown, both dated 16 April 1965, and only 7*d* for the two. The public timetable at this time showed just two trains per week (Monday and Friday) in one direction only from lonely Gatehouse of Fleet to Creetown.

Two more photographs taken on Easter Monday 1963 during the joint SLS/BLS rail tour of south-west Scotland. At Newton Stewart, No. 45588 *Kashmir* was replaced by a lighter locomotive for a trip over the old (and by then freight-only) Wigtownshire Railway. Modern Ivatt Class 2 2-6-0 No 46467 had recently been transferred to Stranraer, especially for duties over this line, but tour participants were hoping for its predecessor, CR 'Jumbo' 0-6-0 No 57375, and they were in luck. Some 244 'Jumbos' were built 1883–97; they were the workhorses of the CR and formed the largest class of Scottish locomotives. A letter to the editor in the July 1943 SLS house magazine said, 'they must be the largest pre-Grouping class extant', with the earliest withdrawal coming in 1946. The first photograph is between Newton Stewart and Wigtown. I was told by our friend R. E. 'Ellis' James-Robertson, who also travelled on this tour, that my father was the only person to get off the train and film here, the gates being opened and then closed by the train crew. Seeing my father's success at not being left behind, enthusiasts piled off the special at the next gates. The second photograph is at Millisle, junction station for the Garlieston branch. The ticket is dated 14 December 1931.

The original objective of what became known as the 'Port Road' was to reach Portpatrick for the short sea crossing to Donaghadee in the north of Ireland, but Portpatrick proved impractical for larger ships and the sheltered harbour at Stranraer was developed instead. Both photographs were taken on Good Friday 1965, the first being at Stranraer Town station. No. 44995 in the bay is ready to take us back to Dumfries at 3.50 p.m., the 'Port Road' being the last line of such a length to still be operated entirely by steam in Scotland. The half-cab DMU behind with a central gangway connection (later Class 126) would work the 4.25 p.m. to Glasgow St Enoch. The track further behind the DMU used to continue on to Portpatrick, to where passenger services ceased in February 1950, after which freight continued to the intermediate station of Colfin until the spring of 1959. Stranraer Town station closed in March 1966; all traffic now uses what used to be called Stranraer Harbour station, but today is just Stranraer. The area between the Town station and the branch to the Harbour station was occupied by extensive sidings and the engine shed complex, part of which is seen in the second photograph.

To take the 1963 Easter 'Scottish Rambler' back to Glasgow from Stranraer on 15 April, two of the four Scottish pre-Grouping veteran locomotives restored to working order in 1959 were used (see pages 6 and 17). The yellow locomotive is HR No. 103, from the first class of 4-6-0 locomotives to run in the British Isles and introduced in 1894. The green locomotive is Great North of Scotland Railway No. 49 *Gordon Highlander*. This was the GNSR's final development of its 4-4-0s; being built after the First World War, No. 49 was kept in first-class condition as it also hauled the Royal train from Aberdeen to Ballater (for Balmoral). The location is Glenwhilly on the line to Girvan that branched off the 'Port Road' at Challoch Junction near Dunragit. A difficult line to build with grades as steep as 1 in 54, it ran through bleak countryside and suffered floods that washed away bridges and embankments. Bogs encountered on the moorland were overcome by supporting the railway on wooden rafts. Construction costs ended up disproportionately high in relation to the returns it might receive; it was in financial trouble from the start and was eventually purchased by the G&SWR.

This is Ayr station, the third for the town and opened by the G&SWR in January 1886. The date is Sunday, 10 April 1966, and 'B1' No. 61342 has charge of another of the SLS/BLS Easter rail tours, having just arrived from Ardrossan. There was a ninety-minute stop here and 'Black 5' No. 44788 is on station pilot duties.

Exchanges of locomotives for comparative testing purposes between the various railway companies did occasionally happen. In 1926, the GWR and LMSR exchanged a 'Castle' and a 'Midland Compound', but it was over two decades later before another exchange took place. In 1948, when the previously independent companies were absorbed into one nationalised system, it was decided to examine the relative capacity and efficiency of the most modern existing classes, and so came about the locomotive exchange of 1948. There was much interest about how particular locomotives would perform and in the mixed-traffic category how the (on paper very similar) 'Black 5' and 'B1' would compare against each other. Author O. S. Nock said that 'the ex-LNER "B1" rather steals the show' and that from his personal observations of the trials between Bristol and Plymouth, he found the 'B1' 'most impressive'.

Above and opposite page: After the demise of BR main line steam in 1968, the National Coal Board (NCB) became the largest user of steam locomotives nationally. The Waterside system in the Ayrshire coalfields was a draw for steam enthusiasts well into the 1970s, and a visit was made here in May 1978, steam finishing later that year. The coal mines in this area originally developed to serve the Dalmellington Iron Company's works at Dunaskin, but the blast furnaces closed in 1921, although the mines continued in production. At Nationalisation in 1947, there was mining at Pennyvenie, Minnivey, and Houldsworth and coal went out along the Dalmellington to Ayr railway, the exchange sidings being next to the washery. In 1963, Ayr became a central collection point for coal shipments to power stations; in places, coal was moving twenty-four hours a day and the rail system was hard-pressed to cope. Two pits survived into the 1970s, Minnivey and Pennyvenie, the latter 3 miles from the washery at Dunaskin. In busier times, four or five steam locomotives could be in use, but as the system declined there was less and less. The last coal was mined out of Minnivey Drift in November 1975 and steam operation finished when Pennyvenie Colliery closed in 1978. In the hills above Waterside, we find No. 24 in the first photograph; this locomotive had been built locally at Kilmarnock by Andrew Barclay (W/N 2235) in 1953. It acquired the Giesl ejector chimney in 1965 to improve steaming and allow poor-quality coal to be used; also note the tender-wagon coupled to it for topping up the locomotive's coal during the shift. It is difficult to read the details in the second photograph, but it is believed to be No. 1, an Andrew Barclay 0-4-0 built in 1955 (W/N 2368). The system also had this steam crane that features in the final photograph. The area is now the site of the Scottish Industrial Railway Centre.

The April 1959 Stephenson Locomotive Society (SLS) monthly journal announced the 'Burns Country Rail Tour' was to be hauled by a CR 3F. However, when the tour actually took place on Saturday, 9 May 1959, it had become the 'Land of Burns Rail Tour' and was instead hauled by Ayr-allocated LMS 2P 4-4-0 No. 40574. Departure from Ayr had been at 1.50 p.m. This is Tarbolton station where the view is looking east; there was a five minutes photo stop here. This was a G&SWR-built line and had opened in 1870 between Ayr and Mauchline. In February 1919, there were only two passenger services eastbound and three westbound on weekdays with no Sunday service. Passenger trains ceased to call at Tarbolton on and from 4 January 1943, although a limited freight service continued until 1 September 1959. Initially, after closure of the 'Port Road' in June 1965, the London Euston to Stranraer 'Northern Irishman' sleeping car service (often 'Britannia'-hauled from Carlisle) was routed through Tarbolton. The line was mothballed in the 1980s but reopened again with an increase in coal traffic; its future must once more be in doubt though with the recent switch away from coal for electricity generation.

Above and next page: Three more photographs taken on the SLS-organised rail tour of Saturday, 9 May 1959. The passenger service through Tarbolton, in the previous commentary, ran between Ayr and Muirkirk, but there was also another G&SWR route between the two towns that opened two years later in 1872. These photographs are all on this later route; it branched off the earlier route at Annbank and rejoined it at Cronberry. The first two views are looking to the south at Drongan. In February 1919, there were two passenger trains each way through Drongan on a service between Ayr and Muirkirk, ceasing in September 1951; however, it was and still is (just) coal traffic that sustained the line. This was a busy location with a passing loop plus water tower, and in the distance, the line split: to the right, Drongan Castle Colliery (by then closed); and to the left, the newly built (and still open) Killoch Colliery line; and straight ahead to (eventually) Muirkirk. My father's notes say of Drongan 'extensive new sidings etc.'. The signal box just visible in the background was a Lancashire and Yorkshire-type and had arrived as a kit of parts; it closed as a block post in July 1975. The third photograph is at Skares, about 6 miles from Drongan towards Muirkirk, where this view is looking to the west. Passenger services also finished here in September 1951 and the line through Skares closed completely in 1966.

The third of the four Scottish pre-Grouping veteran locomotives restored to working order in 1959 seen so far stands at Kilmarnock on 20 April 1962 (and also the date of this ticket). This is CR No. 123 and was built in 1886, achieving fame in the 1888 'Race to the North' when it covered the 100.75 miles from Carlisle to Edinburgh in 102.5 minutes. When withdrawn from normal service in 1935, it was the last working single-wheeler. During the early to mid-Victorian period, there had been considerable railway growth around Kilmarnock, the engine shed established in 1843 adjacent to the station on its north side became inadequate and a new one was built outside the town on a greenfield site at Hurlford in 1873. The old shed is behind CR No. 123 and continued to see some use until around 1960; to its right is a turntable that CR No. 123 has just used. On the opposite side of the station, in what is thought to be May 1959, is 'WD' 2-8-0 No. 90319 standing at one of the two bay platforms.

The G&SWR was formed on 28 October 1850 by the merger of two earlier lines—the Glasgow, Paisley and Kilmarnock Railway and the Glasgow, Dumfries and Carlisle Railway. Earlier in this book (page 22), mention was made of the two original competing railway routes from Carlisle to Glasgow—Annandale (CR) and Nithsdale (the later G&SWR). Despite the fact that the CR 'won' with their route being open throughout by February 1848, the Nithsdale route was not far behind. The two components of the G&SWR met between Cumnock and New Cumnock—GP&KR from the north and GD&CR from the south—completing the through line on 28 October 1850, the same day the G&SWR was formed. A significant difference between the two competing routes was the distance from Carlisle to Glasgow: about 102 miles via the CR, but some 23 miles further by the G&SWR via Dalry.

This view is of New Cumnock station taken on 17 October 1965 looking west with preserved HR No. 103 making its way from Glasgow St Enoch to Dumfries, the last time this locomotive was used before taking up residency in the Glasgow Museum of Transport. The summit of the G&SWR route from Glasgow to Carlisle is close to here and HR No. 103 looks to be making a spirited performance despite hauling only three coaches in poor weather. Noticeable behind the far platform is a very large water tank to feed the water troughs installed by the LMSR to the east of the station.

The author's father labelled these photographs as 'near Muirkirk' and 'colliery branch', so it took some effort before a precise identification was finally achieved. They were taken on the Saturday, 9 May 1959 'Land of Burns Rail Tour' hauled by LMS 2P No. 40574. The location is Lugar, between Auchinleck and Cronberry on the 1848-opened GP&KR route to Muirkirk from Kilmarnock. There was a scheduled five-minute photo stop here. The first photograph is looking towards Muirkirk, the line having been singled about a year previously. The connection going off behind the brick-built cabin connected to a network of lines that served Lugar Iron Works, Lugar Brick Works, and a maze of mineral lines connecting to various local collieries and mines. By 1879, Lugar Iron Works had four furnaces in blast, but it closed in 1926 and was converted into workshops. The second photograph shows the view towards Lugar Iron Works, the line coming in on the left is that going off behind the brick-built cabin in the first. The bridge this photograph is taken from carries the railway the SLS tour train is standing on, while going underneath is the line to Lugar Brick Works.

Above and opposite: On most occasions when we visited Scotland, our base would be with a cousin of my father in Old Coach Road, East Kilbride, and on days when not filming railways, the author enjoyed a trip to the moors around Muirkirk. Little did I know then as a young lad that these moors held hidden treasures underneath them—coal, ironstone, and limestone. Muirkirk Iron Works were established in 1787 and became fully operational by 1796 with three large blast furnaces. The first railway arrived at Muirkirk in 1848 from the west; this fell under G&SWR ownership a couple of years later. The CR cast envious eyes on the riches of Muirkirk from the east and their line arrived in 1873; a second CR route was even constructed from Coalburn but was never opened throughout. Exhaustion of the blackband ironstone seams in 1901 sealed the iron work's fate, with imported Spanish ore keeping things going for a while. The works closed in 1923 following a strike, during which the blast furnaces were allowed to cool with molten iron inside them; coal production continued, however.

The first two photographs are at Muirkirk station with its substantial signal box. They date from the 10 April 1966 visit of the SLS/BLS Easter rail tour with 'B1' No. 61342. The final photograph was taken inside Muirkirk engine shed on 9 May 1959 (the date of this ticket); the CR 'Jumbo' is No. 57353 and unofficially named *Susie*, while the tender on the right is attached to a visiting locomotive from Ardrossan according to my father's notes (see also page 15).

My father travelled to Scotland by rail on 8 May 1959, departing Wolverhampton High Level at 7.46 a.m. for Carstairs, changing at Crewe into the Perth through train with this ticket costing £2 3s 6d. At Carstairs, he took a connecting service to Lanark and then the late afternoon train to Muirkirk, these two photographs both being taken at the last stopping place then still open of Inches. In the first, heading west, the connection to Carmacoup (Kennox) Colliery that had opened in the early twentieth century can be seen branching off. In the distance on this branch, the abutments and railings of a quite substantial girder bridge (which is now a road bridge) across the Douglas Water can just be made out. On return from Muirkirk, in the second photograph, his notes say that he travelled on the locomotive as far as Ponfeigh. The signalman has the single-line token and there are coal wagons in the station goods yard. The railway through Inches closed totally on and from 5 October 1964.

Another two photographs taken on 8 May 1959 (and the date of this ticket to Muirkirk), firstly the signal box at Douglas West station looking to the south-west. The line to Muirkirk opened in 1873 for goods and 1874 for passenger services, although this station did not open until 1896. For a time, the CR ran through trains (not just through coaches) from Edinburgh to Ayr this way and nearby Douglas Castle Colliery supplied the company with locomotive coal. It was 3.25 miles north-east to the next station of Happendon, where the second view is looking towards Lanark. The railway to here from the triangular Smylum Junction near Lanark opened in 1864, this station being called Douglas on opening but Happendon from 1931. Douglas West station was far nearer the actual village of Douglas than was Douglas station, and it must have caused confusion from 1896 before the latter's name change to Happendon in 1931. By the late 1950s, a weekday-only passenger service of four trains each way operated the full distance between Lanark and Muirkirk, with extra Saturday services including an 11.55 p.m. from Lanark that did not arrive at Muirkirk until 12.38 a.m. on the Sunday.

Over the weekend of 15 and 16 October 1965, the Branch Line Society organised a 'Preserved Locomotives Weekend', the last occasion on which either GNSR No. 49 *Gordon Highlander* or HR No. 103 would work before finding a new home at the Glasgow Museum of Transport. Earlier in this book (page 23), we saw the Sunday trip, but the one featured here ran on the Saturday. The author was collected after school on the Friday afternoon in Evesham, Worcestershire, and we flew from Elmdon airport (Birmingham) to Renfrew airport (Glasgow)— the first and only occasion for one of our Scottish trips. By this time, the Lanark to Muirkirk through route had been closed for over a year, but a freight-only service was maintained from the Lanark end to here at Ponfeigh. The station was situated in the village of Douglas Water, which was also known as Ponfeigh and had developed as a coalmining community; the village even once had a bowling green to the rear of the station building. Freight continued until 1968, but today, with the decline of coal mining, the village is now just a ghost of its former self. Our flight back to Birmingham on the Sunday evening was delayed, so the author did not get to school until mid-morning on the Monday and was summoned to the headmaster's office for an explanation; luckily, he was sympathetic.

There used to be two triangular junctions close to Lanark—at Smyllum and Cleghorn/Silvermuir—and sections of both are seen on 8 May 1959. Smyllum East Junction (the one-time Douglas Junction East) is seen on the approach to Lanark from Carstairs, with the single track forking off to the left (opened 1864) allowing direct running towards Muirkirk rather than via reversal at Lanark station. After withdrawal of the Muirkirk passenger service, this track remained in use for freight to Ponfeigh until that ceased in 1968. The second photograph is taken looking back at Silvermuir South Junction on the same train from Carstairs to Lanark, having just passed along the track coming in on the right (opened in 1864) on which the signal is still at 'clear'. This short link was closed in 1968, but its reinstatement has been mooted, allowing a direct passenger service between Lanark and Edinburgh. The tracks heading left here (opened 1854) towards Cleghorn Junction are for Glasgow services to and from Lanark and still in use today, although only single track. Not really visible is the third side of this triangle—the West Coast Main Line—that connects Cleghorn Junction to Silvermuir East Junction.

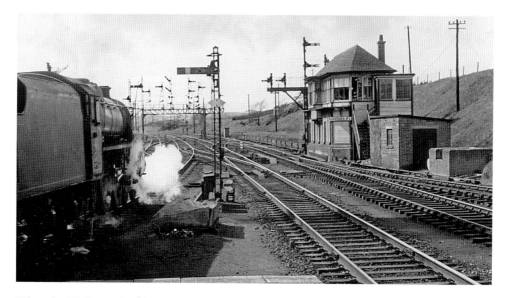

When the CR first arrived here at Carstairs, it was thought of as no more than an isolated country junction with trains running through; instead, carriages from Edinburgh and later Perth were joined at Carstairs to those from Glasgow (the three separate routes of the trident as mentioned in the beginning of this book on page 22). The first photograph was taken at the west end of Carstairs station on 8 May 1959 at just after 3.15 p.m. The morning through service from Crewe to Perth is ready to leave, hauled by Carlisle Kingmoor-allocated 'Black 5' No. 44727 (it had taken over at Carlisle). At the east end of Carstairs during Easter 1965, both D342 and 'Royal Scot' No. 46140 *The King's Royal Rifle Corps* look to be in charge of southbound services. By this time, the number of 'Royal Scots' still in service were in single figures, and they had been banned from working south of Crewe on the electrified main line from September 1964. To indicate this, a yellow diagonal stripe was painted across their cabside numbers, but No. 46140's looks to be completely lost under layers of grime, it would be withdrawn in the coming November.

Above and next page: We called in at Carstairs during our Easter 1962 visit to Scotland when all these three photographs were taken. The end of the CR 0-4-4Ts was by then fast approaching, with the April 1962 *Railway Observer* noting just three still at work. No. 55189 (which features in the first two photographs) survived to the end of the year and was seen on shunting duties in the December, the last class member in regular use; it was preserved thanks to a generous donation from a Worcestershire farmer. By the early 1850s, it was clear that pilot locomotives were often necessary for the long, southbound climb to Beattock summit; thus, an important locomotive depot came to be established at Carstairs. The shed was on the north side of the station and had been comprehensively rebuilt in the mid-1930s, including a mechanical coaling plant. Its shed code after Nationalisation became 64D (66E in June 1960), with steam being removed from the depot in February 1967. With the change from steam to diesel power plus the general contraction of business done by BR in this era, surplus or withdrawn steam locomotives became a common sight all over the network. The location of the final photograph is to the east of the depot, the signalling in the background being for the Edinburgh lines. No. 57583 was a McIntosh-designed CR 3F 0-6-0 that had entered service in 1900 and was withdrawn in November 1961 from Carstairs. The tender in front belongs to 'WD' 2-10-0 No. 90768 (another Carstairs locomotive), which was still in capital stock at this time, withdrawal coming in the July.

The first railway to Coalburn was the 1854-authorised Lesmahagow Railway, a goods and mineral line promoted by local colliery owners and the CR. The line opened in December 1856 and was single throughout. Passenger services started as far as Brocketsbrae (the station for Lesmahagow) in 1866, but it was not until the beginning of November 1891 that this single platform at Coalburn opened for business. Both photographs were taken on 8 May 1959 and the first shows the view south-west towards Bankend Colliery. There was no passenger service on this section, although passenger trains continued towards the colliery to allow locomotives to run around their coaches. Of interest, and only just visible on the extreme left, are two vehicles that will be picked up for loading pigeon crates at Lesmahagow. It was about half a mile to the colliery and the loop can just be made out in the second photograph. The author's father hired a taxi to get from Ponfeigh to Coalburn at a rather costly 10s 0d following his journeys along the Lanark to Muirkirk line seen earlier in this book. Departure from Coalburn was at 7.18 p.m. on the service to Hamilton Central behind No. 77007.

Lanarkshire in pre-Grouping days was virtually a preserve of the CR and they fought tooth and nail to defeat schemes of rival companies to penetrate 'their' area, especially its lucrative coal traffic. The south-west of the county has a complex railway history and here at Lesmahagow, there were two separate routes that paralleled each other for some miles. The 1854-authorised Lesmahagow Railway, a financially independent self-contained unit within the framework of the CR, passed some distance east of Lesmahagow itself. In 1896 and 1897, acts were passed for a number of new CR lines in Mid-Lanarkshire (the Mid-Lanarkshire Extension Lines), including the one in this photograph, which passed much closer to Lesmahagow with a more convenient station location. This new single-track railway, over 8 miles long, was opened by the CR in 1905 and ran from near Stonehouse to Alton Heights Junction, where it joined the existing line to Coalburn.

The first stop on the evening Coalburn to Hamilton Central service on 8 May 1959 was Lesmahagow, but things were delayed here as the vehicles added to the train at Coalburn in the previous commentary had to be loaded with pigeon crates according to my father's notes. This is the view on departure from Lesmahagow station showing the goods yard in which are a substantial number of stored carriages.

A branch of the Lesmahagow Railway was authorised to serve Southfield pit (opened 1856) and extended to the weaving village of Blackwood in 1862 with passenger services starting in 1866. This is the line seen straight ahead in the first photograph at Blackwood Junction taken on 8 May 1959; it had been singled after 28 November 1939 and closed in 1959. The main signal arm is for trains heading behind the photographer to Blackwood station on the 'new' line to Coalburn, the small arm being for trains going to the original Blackwood terminus. Our train is curving to the left on its way to Stonehouse. The second photograph is looking back towards the original 1862 terminus at Blackwood just after passing the town's 1905-opened station on the Mid-Lanarkshire Extension Lines (but not visible). By now, the original terminus was the town's goods depot and also used for carriage storage; until the 1920s, a line continued south to Dunduff quarry. The roof of the original terminus buildings can just be seen above the coaches on the left. The passenger service from Stonehouse and through Blackwood to Coalburn ceased at the beginning of October 1965, although freight carried on to Auchlochan colliery near Coalburn until 1968.

Continuing our evening journey on 8 May 1959 from Coalburn, these two photographs show the arrival at Stonehouse. The first railway here was constructed from Dalserf Junction on the Lesmahagow Railway and passed through Stonehouse to terminate at Cot Castle for a total distance of 4 miles and 42 chains. This line opened in 1864 with passenger services starting two years later (though Cot Castle remained goods only). The Lesmahagow Railway largely avoided the towns, and one of the purposes of the CR Mid-Lanarkshire Extension Lines Acts was to remedy this. A line was built south from Merryton Junction (a few miles from Hamilton) to join the 1864-built railway already at Stonehouse and then onwards to Alton Heights Junction (and Coalburn), this opening in 1905. Thus, Stonehouse ended up with four converging routes—Dalserf Junction, Alton Heights Junction, Cot Castle, and Merryton Junction. In the first photograph, the diverging routes beyond Stonehouse signal box (originally Stonehouse West) are left along the route we have just travelled—Blackwood, Lesmahagow, Alton Heights Junction, and Coalburn, or straight on to Cot Castle and Strathaven (since 1905). The bay platform on the left in the second photograph was used for any connecting service to Strathaven, while in the distance are the diverging routes.

These two photographs show views at the other end of Stonehouse station on 8 May 1959. In the first looking to the north-east, although only a small portion of the locomotive is visible, noticeable is the very high running plate; it is BR Standard Class 3 2-6-0 No. 77007 and allocated to Hamilton at this time. The signal is clear for a scheduled 7.50 p.m. departure and the track can be seen curving left. There used to be a line curving right; this was the first railway at Stonehouse, from Dalserf Junction to Cot Castle. This line had closed in 1935 and, after closure, the signal box at this end of the station (Stonehouse East) was demolished. My father's notes comment on the neatness of the station and on the far platform are what could be more pigeon crates. The view in the second photograph on the other side of the train shows the overgrown trackbed around the island platform; as with the Stonehouse East signal box, the rails here were removed following closure of the line to Dalserf Junction in 1935. The passenger service to Stonehouse and onwards to both Strathaven and Coalburn ceased at the beginning of October 1965.

Around the Stonehouse area, everything authorised by the Mid-Lanarkshire Extension Lines Acts of 1896 and 1897 were all constructed with one exception. A railway had been approved under the 1896 Act that was to run from the Lanarkshire/Ayrshire border near Darvel via Strathaven to Cot Castle, whence it would turn to the south-west near Stonehouse and continue to Blackwood Junction. The junction near Cot Castle was never laid in, but the double track to what would have been the junction with the line from Coalburn to Stonehouse was. However, the physical junction of the tracks was never completed and it was instead accessed by a shunting spur from Stonehouse West signal box running parallel to the Coalburn line; the spur was used for storage of stock.

The G&SWR were trying to expand Troon as a coal-exporting port as an alternative to the congestion at Glasgow docks, but by the time the line from Strathaven to Darvel opened for goods and mineral traffic in June 1904, the docks at Glasgow had been considerably enlarged and could cope with the Lanarkshire coal. Had the junctions at both ends of this never fully completed spur at Stonehouse been laid in, the G&SWR could probably have claimed running powers for coal traffic that the CR wanted to keep to themselves. Taken from a moving train on its way to Stonehouse from Coalburn and dating from 8 May 1959, this view shows the remains of the spur; the bridge carries the road from Stonehouse to Strathaven.

The final intermediate stopping place on our evening journey from Coalburn towards Hamilton using this 8 May 1959 ticket was Larkhall, a place that bore similarities in its early days to Lesmahagow. The 1856-opened Lesmahagow Railway ran to the east of Larkhall and the station on the LR line (opened for passengers in 1866) was not particularly well-sited for the town. This is a view of Larkhall goods yard on the 1905-opened line from Merryton Junction to Stonehouse and Coalburn. The station at Larkhall on this line was called Larkhall Central, whereas that on the old Lesmahagow Railway was called Larkhall East (closed to passengers in 1951). The goods yard was on the east side of the track and to the south of Larkhall Central station, while prominent in the distance, is the spire of St Machan's Parish Church.

Larkhall Central station closed on and from 4 October 1965 and freight ceased in November 1968 with the closure of the last colliery along the route. However, Larkhall station (without the Central) has been born again; it reopened on 12 December 2005 and is now on the Glasgow electrified system.

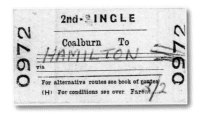

Above and opposite: Three more photographs dating from my father's visit to Scotland during early May 1959, all being taken at High Blantyre. The Hamilton and Strathaven Railway was authorised in 1857 from Strathaven Junction, 60 chains north-west of the terminus at Hamilton (the later Hamilton West); it followed a circuitous route via Meikle Earnock and Glassford to Strathaven. The line was open for goods as far as the strangely named Quarter Road on 6 June 1860, and throughout for passenger and goods traffic on 2 February 1863. The H&SR was worked from the start by the CR and was vested in them during 1864. By 1906, there were nine though passenger trains daily with three extra on Saturdays; most passengers from Strathaven had to change at Hamilton if travelling to Glasgow. There was no passenger service on Sundays. The line also served numerous industrial sites, such as collieries, quarries, and Quarter Iron Works. However, by the end of the Second World War, things had changed; the passenger service was withdrawn in September 1945 and eight years later, all the coal mines beyond High Blantyre had been closed. All workings between High Blantyre and Strathaven ceased in September 1953 and the section was abandoned.

By the date of these photographs, the only part still open was from Strathaven Junction, Hamilton, to here at High Blantyre; this finished one year later at the beginning of June 1960. Things look very run-down in the first photograph, looking to the north, with High Blantyre station in the distance and the signal box on the left. At one time, the line was double track and the evidence can be seen in the second photograph, showing the continuation behind High Blantyre station, with this bridge crossing the East Kilbride Road. Barely visible in the middle distance on the left and in front of the houses is an embankment that once carried the already-closed railway to East Kilbride, the two routes joining at Hunthill Junction. The final photograph shows a close-up around the nameplate of High Blantyre signal box.

On page 46 in a photograph taken during Easter 1965, we saw a very run-down 'Royal Scot' class locomotive approaching the end of its life. Two years earlier during Easter 1963 found us at Glasgow Central, and while this 'Royal Scot' does not look in tip-top condition, it certainly looks anything but run-down. It is No. 46156 *The South Wales Borderer* and heading a relief to the southbound 'Royal Scot' express. This is a rebuilt class member; in fact, all had been rebuilt for some years by 1963 and were giving excellent service. In the gloom of early post-war locomotive and train performance, the work of the 'Rebuilt Royal Scots' shone brightly, and they were acclaimed as the most outstanding British 4-6-0s. In deference to GWR enthusiasts, the 'Kings' were yet to receive four-row superheaters and double chimneys, but even then, their heavier weight restricted their route availability relative to that of the 'Royal Scots'. Of interest at this time was the AC overhead electrification, only energised the year previously at Glasgow Central for the Cathcart Circle Line. However, it is not at the usual 25 kV; it is instead at 6.25 kV to lower the risk of electrical flashover, the EMUs having switchable transformers to maintain the same power at the lower voltage. The 6.25-kV system was converted to the standard 25 kV in the early 1970s.

Over the years, we travelled on a lot of special trains, two of which it has been said represented some of the most epic locomotive performances of all time. The first was on 9 May 1964, the 'Great Western' high speed trip from London Paddington to Plymouth and back. However, this photograph relates to the second—the Railway Correspondence and Travel Society's (RCTS) 'Scottish Lowlander' tour on 26 September 1964; included is my child ticket. It had started from Crewe with the last ever pre-preservation working of a Stanier 'Coronation Pacific', No. 46256 *Sir William A. Stanier, F.R.S.*—rather appropriately the one named after the designer himself. It is nearly 5 p.m. and the tour locomotive by this time was the now-preserved 'A4' No. 60009 *Union of South Africa*. The author remembers this as a location towards the centre of Glasgow called St John's, where, unusually, the locomotive had to uncouple from the train to be able to fill up its tender with water. It is only in more recent years that I have been able to track down the precise spot. St John's signal box was about half a mile from the G&SWR terminus at St Enoch, and near to the 1902-closed station of Gallowgate. On departure after our water stop, No. 60009 continued along the City of Glasgow Union Railway, a through line from the north-east to the south-west of Glasgow that included a four-track bridge over the Clyde, and then onwards towards Kilmarnock.

The SLS/BLS 'Scottish Rambler No. 4' rail tour on 17 April 1965 (Easter Saturday) travelled over a number of freight-only lines in the Paisley area with preserved HR No. 103. The author, despite taking both photographs, could not remember exactly where the first was—surely that block of flats would aid precise identification, but no. Thanks go to my wife Barbara's cousin, Jeff Sedgley, who lived in Paisley for a time and was able to provide a location. The locomotive is propelling its train from Paisley West over the G&SWR freight-only branch to Potterhill, on which passenger services had ceased during the First World War. The block of flats is along Corsebar Road close to an entrance for the Hospital; freight continued on the Potterhill branch until 1970 serving a Cadbury's depot. The second location was on the branch to the home of Hillman 'Imp' cars: Linwood. This freight-only branch (not the one that served the actual car factory) turned off the CR line from Paisley to Gourock at Blackstone Junction; it had opened in 1882 and originally served a colliery but never had a passenger service and closed in 1967.

The earliest steamships in the world plied their trade upon the Firth of Clyde and a near-fleet of privately owned ships sailed from the heart of Glasgow to numerous jetties along the Firth and the islands. With the coming of the Glasgow, Paisley and Greenock Railway in 1841 (CR from 1851), a new factor entered the competition on the Clyde. Combined rail and steamer services offered the inducement of speed in getting from Glasgow to Dunoon, Rothesay, or further afield. In 1865, the Greenock and Ayrshire Railway (G&SWR from 1872) obtained authority for another line to Greenock that would have the great advantage over the CR of a terminal station at the water's edge. Both photographs are taken along this now-closed G&SWR route on 17 April 1965 with the same tour hauled by HR No. 103, firstly, passing Houston and Crosslee station and then just after arrival at Greenock Princes Pier. The CR responded with a costly 1889-opened extension to Gourock, a good 3 miles further downstream. Competition remained intense; in the thirty minutes after 4 p.m., eleven boat trains were dispatched from the Glasgow termini, these connecting with thirteen steamers.

Above and next three pages: The final place in Scotland where regular commercially operated working steam locomotives could be found was R. B. Tennent's foundry at Whifflet, Coatbridge. All these photographs date from a visit to the premises during May 1978, with steam operations lasting here until 1984 (a fireless locomotive survived at Ardrossan refinery until 1986). The company had been established in 1857 and quickly grew to be the largest roll-making unit in the UK; at its height, the foundry produced 40 per cent of the country's chilled cast-iron rolls and 60 per cent of the cast-iron rolls.

The company did not use the conventional type of steam locomotive. These Sentinel locomotives have vertical boilers and are chain driven, the Sentinel Company beginning in 1913 as Alley and MacLellan and based at Polmadie, Glasgow. A move was made to Shrewsbury in 1915, and it became the Sentinel Waggon Works (1920) Ltd. In the 1920s and '30s, they led the market for steam-powered road vehicles and used the technology to produce this kind of steam shunting locomotive; Tennent's eventually had four of the type.

First seen is *Ranald* and built in 1957 (W/N 9627). It arrived here around November 1969 from the Rugby Portland Cement Co. Ltd, Rochester Works, Halling, Kent. Secondly, *Robin* (W/N 9628) was built in 1957 and came brand new to Tennent's. Thirdly, *John* (W/N 9561) had been built in 1953 and arrived at Tennent's during January 1960; it was previously Sentinel's demonstration locomotive. *Denis* (W/N 9631 and formerly named *The Doctor*) dated from 1958 and arrived from Miller and Co. Ltd of Edinburgh around March 1963 (see introductory photograph on page 17). As can be seen, there were also plenty of spare parts for them lying around the works.

Both photographs were taken looking north at Glenboig station on a rather wet 5 June 1965, although the station itself had closed in June 1956. At the other end of the platform was the important junction of Garnqueen North where the main line split west to Glasgow Buchanan Street or south to England. By 1866, the CR had either built or taken over other railways so that it owned virtually the entire route from Carlisle to Aberdeen—a main line some 241 miles long plus a snug monopoly in much of Angus and the Mearns. However, the 52 chains south of Garnqueen South Junction became a curious anomaly in British railway geography. This section had been constructed by the Monkland and Kirkintilloch Railway, which was absorbed by the North British Railway, one of the CR's great rivals, although a working arrangement was agreed between the two opposing parties. This continued until Nationalisation, with the CR becoming part of the LMSR and the NBR part of the LNER at the Grouping. In the first photograph, 'A4' No. 60007 *Sir Nigel Gresley* is bound for Glasgow Buchanan Street, but D336 in the second is heading for England. (*Alan Maund*)

Above and next page: Close to Glenboig was another location where working steam locomotives could still be found well into the 1970s; these three photographs date from a visit to Bedlay Colliery during May 1978. William Baird and Co. opened this colliery in 1905, which was established to provide high-quality coking coal for Gartsherrie Iron Works. By 1969, it employed about 1,000 people and produced some 250,000 tons annually. The oldest locomotive was 0-6-0 No. 9, a Hudswell Clarke product of 1909 (W/N 895), seen in the first two photographs. It was the most popular locomotive at Bedlay and often worked to the BR exchange sidings about 1 mile away on the old Monkland and Kirkintilloch Railway. Withdrawal for No. 9 came in 1979 following foundation ring problems in the firebox, but it still survives at the Summerlee Museum of Scottish Industrial Life, Coatbridge. The 0-4-0 No. 17 features in the first and last photographs; it had been built by Andrew Barclay in 1950 (W/N 2296) and was transferred to Bedlay in June 1973 after overhaul. There were no facilities for the locomotives here and they were serviced and stored in the open. Winding of coal ceased at Bedlay in December 1981, by which time the site had become the last to use conventional steam locomotives on a regular commercial basis in Scotland with No. 17 being the last locomotive; Bedlay was also the last deep mine in the Monklands. No. 17 survived to be transferred to Barony Colliery, Ayrshire, where it was spare to the diesel fleet. When Barony closed in 1989, No. 17 was the last steam locomotive owned by the British Coal Corporation (successor to the NCB) and was donated to the Scottish Railway Preservation Society at Bo'ness.

In my first book covering the railways of Scotland, *Steam Trails—Scottish Lowlands and Borders*, I wanted to use two particular photographs taken by our friend the late Alan Maund. Sadly, Alan did not leave any details regarding location or date, and, despite extensive research, I could not identify them. Eventually, I started showing the photographs at the beginning of my film shows around the country and asking if anyone could recognise them; success came at a show for the Festiniog Railway Society. The photographs were taken close to Lennoxtown. These two photographs are of that same Lennoxtown-bound freight train and while I cannot precisely identify the location of the first, the second is approaching the level crossing by Rowantree Terrace on the B822. The locomotive is 'J37' No. 64613 and allocated to St Margaret's, Edinburgh, around the time of this photograph, which I suspect to be about 1961. The last passenger trains to Lennoxtown ran at the end of September 1951, but freight carried on until the beginning of April 1966. (*Alan Maund*)

Above and opposite: A TV programme the author enjoyed on Sunday evenings in the 1960s was *Dr. Finlay's Casebook*, parts of which were filmed in the town of Callander (the fictional Tannochbrae) that features in these three photographs. Despite there being schemes for railways through the Highlands of Scotland dating from the 'Railway Mania' of around 1845, it took some years to become a reality. Trying to make the economics add up was a big problem—any railway would be difficult and expensive to build, added to which the population was often sparse or non-existent for considerable distances; plus, there was little in the way of mineral wealth. The Dunblane, Doune and Callander Railway obtained its act in 1846, but capital dried up following the 'Railway Mania' and the scheme was dropped. It was revived ten years later with the Scottish Central Railway (CR from 1866) being persuaded to part-finance the project with the thought that it could become the starting point for a line into the Highlands. The railway to Callander from Dunblane opened at the beginning of July 1858, was worked by the SCR, and was absorbed by them in 1865. It did indeed become the starting point for a line westwards, with the Callander and Oban Railway being authorised in 1865. The distance was over 70 miles and a shortage of funds meant the C&OR opened in stages and did not reach Oban until 1880. The original DD&CR terminus at Callander closed in 1870 (becoming a goods depot) when this station opened on the initial stage of the line further west. The first photograph shows single-wheeler CR No. 123 on Good Friday 1963, hauling the SLS/BLS 'Scottish Rambler No. 2' rail tour in a view looking east. The other two photographs date from July 1963 and show the view looking west; No. 42168 (see also page 8) had arrived on a terminating local service and wold soon head back towards Stirling. (*Second and third photos: Alan Maund*)

There was not much indication in the previous photograph at Callander on Good Friday 1963 as to the change in weather CR No. 123 would experience by the time it arrived here at Killin Junction (ticket included) some 19 miles further on (see also page 13). In between the two stations, the train had climbed to a height of about 940 feet up Glen Ogle, involving gradients as steep as 1 in 60 for over 4 miles, hauling its two preserved CR coaches. Despite its claim to fame in the 1888 'Race to the North', CR No. 123 was soon superseded by more powerful types; the days of single-wheelers were over and more adhesive weight was needed to cope with heavier trains. Regular jobs in later years were hauling the directors' saloon and as pilot to the Royal Train. It was kept in impeccable condition after withdrawal in 1935 at St Rollox shed, Glasgow, until 1957, when, inspired by the success of restoring GWR 4-4-0 *City of Truro* to working order, the same was done for CR No. 123. Four Scottish pre-Grouping locomotives were ultimately restored to working order for the September 1959 Scottish Industries Exhibiiton held in the Kelvin Hall, Glasgow. CR No. 123 did not just haul special trains in Scotland; on 15 September 1963, it worked a tour from London Victoria to Haywards Heath, Sussex, and back, with the authorities even painting the coal white to try and keep the locomotive in tip-top external condition. The roughly 40 miles of railway from Dunblane to Crianlarich was closed throughout in 1965, with Oban now being reached via the West Highland Line to Crianlarich instead.

Glenoglehead summit on the line west from Callander is only some 3 miles away from Killin, but a height difference of about 570 feet precluded the railway to Oban directly passing through the village. Instead, a locally promoted line was built, with the Killin Railway Company being incorporated in 1883. To avoid excessive gradients, a trailing connection with the main line at Killin Junction was made after the latter had descended some way from Glenoglehead summit; even so, the branch dropped steeply. It opened to both Killin and the pier on Loch Tay in 1886. Good main line connections were the norm and combined excursions were run in conjunction with steamers on the Loch. Although operated by the CR, the company was not absorbed until the Grouping. Both photographs are of the Good Friday 1963 special, firstly at Loch Tay and then Killin itself on the way back. The branch locomotive was No. 80093 and from Killin Junction, the special took the place of a normal service train. Regular passenger services at Loch Tay had ceased in September 1939, but the small engine shed was here (page 15); the branch closed in 1965.

The 1865-authorised Callander and Oban Railway's financial affairs were in a sorry plight and it took fifteen years before the line reached the coast. Glenoglehead (named Killin until 1886) was reached in 1870, Tyndrum in 1873, and here at Dalmally in 1877. It must not be forgotten that even before the 1870s, it was possible to reach Oban from Glasgow in 9.75 hours by boat via the Crinan Canal. The CR must have looked on at its floundering *protégé* with dismay as a rival concern further north, the Dingwall and Skye Railway (backed by the Highland Railway and also authorised in 1865), was through to Strome Ferry by August 1870 with connecting steamer services starting immediately. However, the C&OR had only reached Glenoglehead. Both photographs were taken from the same road bridge to the west of Dalmally station and both have a Kodak date stamp of July 1963. The siding on the south side of the station and to the right of the departing diesel used to be the site of a small engine shed plus turntable. The semaphore signalling was replaced at Dalmally in 1986 by Radio Electronic Token Block (RETB) signalling. (*Alan Maund*)

The opening of the about 100-mile-long West Highland Railway from Craigendoran to Fort William in 1894 gave notice to railways serving the west coast of Scotland to up their game. Parliamentary sanction was obtained to improve steamer berthing facilities at Oban and also to construct a single-line branch from Connel Ferry (about 6 miles from Oban) through the Appin coastal district to Ballachulish. The cost of this branch proved out of proportion to the traffic immediately on offer, the area being little more than a remote and depopulated stretch of West Highland wilderness. It was 27.75 miles long and opened to here at Ballachulish in 1903—very late in the day for such a long railway. By the date of these July 1963 photographs, steam was a thing of the past. The number of the diesel that looks to be running around its train is difficult to read, but it appears to be in the D534x series. There were proposals for a railway north to Fort William (only 15 miles away), even through the Great Glen to Inverness, but they came to nothing. Ballachulish closed to all traffic at the end of March 1966. (*Alan Maund*)

Above and opposite: Tuesday, 7 August 1894 saw the opening for service of the West Highland Railway, with a ceremonial opening following four days later. The railway stretched through 100 miles of mountain and moorland from Craigendoran to Fort William (with a later extension to Mallaig) with not a branch line or scarcely a village of any size in all its length. The *Railway Herald* even likened the area traversed to previously unknown parts of Central Africa. Despite the best efforts of the CR, the North British Railway had absorbed the Edinburgh and Glasgow Railway in 1865 and so gained access towards the west of Scotland. Now, the NBR triumphed again, through its foster child, the WHR, penetrating deep into CR territory. The WHR was a railway within a railway with its own board of directors and its own capital; the NBR undertook to staff and work the line with its own men, engines, and rolling stock. The NBR guaranteed a 3.5 per cent dividend to WHR shareholders and contributed £150,000 for this extension of its influence. Knowing the rather meagre prizes to be had in the area, the Highland Railway was apprehensive the WHR would harm its own hard-won line over the Grampians to Inverness; equally, the CR feared a possible threat to its subordinate the C&OR. When the WHR 1894 ceremonial train approached Fort William, it passed the first houses in the first town for 100 miles; the moment Fort William had been waiting for half a century had come at last.

There had been earlier proposals of which the Glasgow and North Western Railway bill presented to Parliament in 1882 was probably the grandest ever in the UK. This was to be 167 miles long from Glasgow to Inverness via Loch Lomond, Rannoch Moor, Glencoe, and Fort William, including 19 miles of dead-level track (partly on a causeway) alongside Loch Ness.

Today, although the line still provides a service for the local community in the West Highlands, it is the scenic delights that are widely promoted and these three photographs show typical views. First is believed to be by the side of Loch Lomond with the 'Jacobite' special train heading north on 1 June 1963. Second is an unknown location among the rugged hills and moorland, believed to date from about 1961. Finally, the Inner Hebrides can be glimpsed in the distance nearing Mallaig on 1 June 1963. My child ticket for the 'Jacobite' organised by the Scottish Locomotive Preservation Fund is included; this was advertised as 'likely to be the last steam train over the entire length of the WHR'. (*Second photo: Alan Maund*)

From Bridge of Orchy, the WHR struck north into barren and roadless country. The 30 miles to Inverlair (Tulloch) involved crossing some of the most desolate country in Europe, and in the middle of it was Rannoch Moor. The scenery changed perceptibly with every mile passed—trees vanished, vegetation other than heather and scrub became scarcer, and civilisation was left behind. After 8 miles of steady climbing, the isolated WHR outpost of Gorton (Gortan previous to 1 May 1926) was reached at a height of around 1,100 feet. There was a signal box and house for the signalman plus his family, and in the late 1930s, an old carriage body was placed on the platform to serve as a school. The first photograph (with snow still on the peaks) shows the 'Jacobite' rail tour on 1 June 1963 at Gorton on its way north. 'J37' No. 64632 had overheated and was being removed by preserved NBR No. 256 *Glen Douglas* (see also page 13). The second photograph, thought to date from about 1961, shows what appears to be an engineering train heading towards Bridge of Orchy, with the old 'school' visible on Gorton's platform. (*Second photo: Alan Maund*)

The 'Jacobite' rail tour on 1 June 1963 had been organised by the Scottish Locomotive Preservation Fund and was to be the last (pre-preservation) steam-hauled train over the full length of the WHR to Mallaig and back. To cope with the grades, the nine-coach train was to be double-headed throughout. However, with only NBR No. 256 *Glen Douglas* now in sole charge after Gorton, a major problem was the grade of 1 in 53 ahead of the train in the first photograph at Rannoch. Assistance was required and it eventually came in the form of D6137, with tour participants thronging over the tracks in the meantime, enjoying the sunny weather and scenery. Rannoch was something of an oasis on the moor to house and shelter the railwaymen who serviced this lonely section of line. While visitors might have marvelled at the location, shareholders must have worried where on earth the traffic would come from to make the line pay. The second photograph is at the south end of Rannoch station in about 1961 and shows a freight train hauled by a 'Black 5' ready to head towards Gorton. (*Second photo: Alan Maund*)

Alan Maund did not date any of the photographs he took along the West Highland line, but as the numbers of the locomotives are visible in these two shots taken at Fort William, it is possible to close in on the time period a little. 'K1' No. 62011 is at the west end of the original terminus at Fort William; it was locally allocated until the beginning of December 1962, after which it survived around Tyneside until the very end of steam workings there in September 1967. 'B1' No 61352 is at the other end of Fort William station and was transferred here in the summer of 1961; it is displaying the shed code used at Fort William (63B) from the summer of 1960. No. 61352 was inter-regionally transferred to Gorton (the Gorton at Manchester, not the isolated passing place on the edge of Rannoch Moor) in September 1962 and withdrawn that October. This station was closed in June 1975; it was replaced by a new one some distance to the north-east and close to where the engine shed used to be, with the A82 main road now largely following the old track bed. (*Alan Maund*)

The WHR as originally planned was to have a terminal on the coast at Roshven that would have been close to the fishing villages, and a pier was to be built for island steamers; Fort William was nearly 100 miles away by boat from the fishing grounds (40 miles overland). A 'Road to the Isles' was eventually agreed and the first sod of the Mallaig Extension was cut at Corpach on 21 January 1897. Earlier, a branch 1.75 miles long had opened in 1895 from just east of Fort William to Banavie on the banks of the Caledonian Canal, with the WHR hoping to establish trade with vessels plying the canal. The Mallaig Extension started from along this earlier branch. An initial challenge was crossing the canal. A swing bridge was provided and seen in both of these August 1970 photographs that are looking towards Mallaig. The bridge is pivoted on one bank to leave the whole channel clear for shipping; it was operated by hand and is still used today. This old signal box was replaced by the Banavie signalling centre in 1987, using the RETB system; except for some local movements, it controls the entire West Highland line plus also that to Oban.

Two more photographs from what was thought would be the last ever steam train over the Mallaig Extension—the 'Jacobite' rail tour on 1 June 1963. Following the locomotive problem earlier that day (pages 13 and 78) when 'J37 No. 64632 had to be left behind at the remote outpost of Gorton, two fresh 'J37s' (especially worked up earlier from the south as regular steam had already ceased), Nos 64636 and 64592, were to haul the train from Fort William to Mallaig and back. A report in the *Railway Observer* around this time noted only one out-of-use and withdrawn steam locomotive at Fort William—No. 44255, the one-time snow-plough engine. Bridges on the Mallaig Extension were built of concrete, most of them in standard spans of 50 feet. The most spectacular was at Glenfinnan in the first photograph; it used twenty-one standard spans with a total length of 1,248 feet on a 12-chain radius curve and reached a maximum height above the ground of 100 feet. Grades on the extension are steeper than on the 100 miles to Fort William, the climb away from Glenfinnan Station in the second photograph involving a section at 1 in 45.

Locomotive problems were a major feature of the 'Jacobite' tour on 1 June 1963 from Glasgow Queen Street to Mallaig and back. Due to the route's NBR heritage, it was arranged that four NBR locomotives would haul the train, but as the company had ceased to exist at the 1923 Grouping, this meant a minimum individual age of some forty years. The locomotives used on the Glasgow to Fort William stage were 'J37' No. 64632 (left behind on the edge of Rannoch Moor after failure) and preserved NBR No. 256 *Glen Douglas* (declared a failure on arrival at Fort William). The author recalls seeing impressive lineside fires on the hills by the side of Loch Lomond on our return to Glasgow and was told the *Glen Douglas* had been the cause on these on the outbound journey. Arisaig had opened in 1901 on the Mallaig Extension and an extended stop was made here; as can be seen, 'J37' No. 64592 was being investigated by train crew. This locomotive and classmate No. 64636 behind had taken over at Fort William and by the time we arrived at Mallaig, both were apparently declared failures. With no steam locomotives left in working order, the return to Glasgow was by diesel, with D5351 hauling the train throughout with arrival at Queen Street after midnight. My father, whose ticket for this special train is included, used to say the tour would have done much better had modern steam locomotives been used rather than NBR types—the benefit of hindsight. Yet how things have changed; the 1 June 1963 'Jacobite' rail tour did not prove to be the last steam train to Mallaig. Today (and, in fact, for many years now), regular 'tourist' steam-hauled trains run between Fort William and Mallaig.

At the beginning of August 1969, the author and his school friend each purchased one of these BR national Rail Rover tickets valid for one week. One of our journeys was on the overnight train from London Kings Cross that provided a through service to Mallaig over the full length of the West Highland Line. At Mallaig, the train from Kings Cross connected with boat services and we caught the MacBrayne's steamer to Kyle of Lochalsh.

In July 1865, powers were granted for the 65-mile-long Dingwall and Skye Railway to reach the west coast. As originally planned, the idea was to pass through Strathpeffer Spa on the way, whose mineral springs were already well known; however, local landowners put up determined opposition. A further act was obtained three years later, sanctioning various deviations; Strathpeffer was now passed some 2 miles to its north, and at the west end of the line, the section onwards from Strome Ferry to Kyle of Lochalsh was abandoned because of its high cost. The result of the latter was to move the terminus 10 miles up the seawater Loch Carron to Strome Ferry that was not such a good harbour as Kyle of Lochalsh due to strong currents and tides. The railway to Strome Ferry opened in August 1870 with connecting steamers also starting to Portree on Skye and to Stornoway on Lewis. In June 1893, the Highland Railway obtained a further act for the extension from Strome Ferry to Kyle of Lochalsh and to provide a pier there. This was done to compete against the WHR, who would open to Fort William in 1894 and seemed likely to extend westwards. Civil engineering was heavy for this extension that wound in and out along the shore through a series of deep rock cuttings; it opened at the beginning of November 1897. This undated photograph, taken on the extension from Strome Ferry, shows the train is bound for Kyle of Lochalsh and includes an observation car at the rear. (*Alan Maund*)

In 1845, a prospectus was issued for a direct line across the mountains from Nairn to Perth, the engineer being Joseph Mitchell (assistant to Thomas Telford on Highland road construction). Mitchell was ridiculed in Parliament with comparisons to Hannibal and the proposed railway was rejected. The year 1860 saw more talk of a shorter railway to the south rather via Aberdeen that was both longer and inconvenient (the GNSR and CR systems at Aberdeen were not rail-linked until 1867).Mitchell's services were again called upon, this time with a route south from Forres that for much of its length still followed the 1845 proposal. Locomotive technology had advanced since 1845, and while still characterised by steep grades, opponents were unable to stop the Bill this time and it passed on 22 July 1861. One result was that Druimuachdar (Gaelic) became the highest summit on a standard-gauge line in Britain at 1,484 feet. The two photographs (see also page 19) are both labelled as Drumochter (Anglicised) July 1963, but none of the diesels are identified. The uphill combination includes a later 'Class 40' with a possible horse box as the first vehicle; the building is believed to be Edendon box (closed December 1951). (*Alan Maund*)

Alan Maund and Wendy Waddoup married near Worcester in August 1962. In July 1963, they toured Scotland and Wendy is seen by the side of 'The Orcadian' at Inverness; all the photographs over the next few pages along the Far North Line to Thurso being taken at this time.

The first line to serve the capital of the Highlands was the Inverness and Nairn Railway, with powers being obtained in July 1854 for a railway 15 miles long, heading east. The first sod was cut in September 1854 and it was hoped to have the line ready for opening by the beginning of August 1855, but with all major equipment having to be brought in by sea, delays were inevitable and the date proved to be 5 November 1855. Soon after opening, thoughts turned northwards and the Inverness and Ross-shire Railway opened to Dingwall in June 1862, this line heading due west though for some miles because of the Beauly Firth. However, the station at Inverness had been built for the railway heading east to Nairn and could not be converted to a through station. It was decided to enlarge the existing station by provision of extra terminal platforms on the west side to accommodate the Ross-shire trains. The two routes diverged immediately beyond the station passing on either side of what was then the locomotive works at Lochgorm. The third side of this triangle of lines ran from east to west and was formed by part of the harbour branch and is known as the Rose Street curve. The coaches in the background are on the original route out of the station to Nairn, while the unidentified diesel hauling 'The Orcadian' is standing on the sharply curved track added in 1862. (*Alan Maund*)

The Inverness and Ross-shire Railway in the previous commentary (following amalgamation with the Inverness and Aberdeen Junction Railway) extended to close by the Sutherland border, arriving at Bonar Bridge (renamed Ardgay from 1977) on 1 October 1864. These next two photographs are both in Sutherland and date from July 1963. The Sutherland Railway (SR) was authorised on 29 June 1865 to construct a railway from Bonar Bridge to Brora (a distance of 32.75 miles), with the HR contributing £15,000. The section from Bonar Bridge to Golspie opened on 13 April 1868 with a connecting coach service to the north. The first photograph is the view to the south at Lairg with oil tanks visible in the goods yard, a service that has only recently ceased. Golspie is seen in the second photograph with the northbound 'Orcadian' at the platform, the brick piers to the right once supported a water tower for replenishing steam locomotives. The September 1961 issue of *Modern Railways* reported only one steam engine active north of Inverness: GWR-designed 0-6-0 tank engine No. 1649 at Dingwall. (*Alan Maund*)

The SR had stopped short at Golspie instead of building through to Brora as authorised. The next advance to the north was courtesy of the Duke of Sutherland, the principle landowner in the county, and he planned a privately owned line along the coast for about 17 miles to Helmsdale. The act authorising transfer of the 6 miles of SR line from Golspie to Brora plus the extension from Brora to Helmsdale was passed on 20 June 1870, although construction had begun before powers were obtained. Engineering difficulties at either end delayed completion, but from here at Dunrobin (about 2 miles north of Golspie) to just short of Helmsdale was finished by the autumn of 1870; the Duke decided this section should be opened at once. An engine and coaches were purchased, but with the line being physically isolated from the national network these were hauled by traction engine along the road. With the full opening of the entire route, the temporary terminus at Dunrobin became a private station serving the castle and, in 1902, the buildings were reconstructed as in this July 1963 photograph. Visible at the northern end of the platform is the shed, which formerly housed the Duke's private saloon; his locomotive was kept initially at Brora, but later Golspie. The station closed in 1965 but reopened in 1985 and is now called Dunrobin Castle; it is no longer a private station as the general public are able to use it. (*Alan Maund*)

The first station opened by the Duke of Sutherland at West Helmsdale was open for less than a year from 1 November 1870. The Helmsdale station that features in both of these July 1963 photographs looking to the north opened on 19 June 1871, with the HR taking over working the entire line at the same time (Dunrobin also becoming a private station). Contracts for carrying the Royal Mail were an important source of revenue for many railways in Britain, and there certainly seems to be brisk business being done on this July 1963 day with D5337 engaging in some shunting. In 1901, the HR were able to keep the mail contract (worth £27,000) between Skye and the mainland despite the opening of a competitive route to Mallaig. It is still valuable today; in January 2017, Loganair secured a five-year contract to fly mail throughout Scotland. The GWR-designed lightweight tank engines that were transferred hundreds of miles to Scotland in the 1950s for working the Dornoch branch were allocated here at Helmsdale; their new home, the long-closed engine shed, was adjacent to the platform these photographs are taken from. (*Alan Maund*)

Above and opposite: Looking at a map of the area between Inverness and Wick, it is immediately obvious the railway follows a rather indirect route. The tracks go around rather than across the Moray (Beauly), Cromarty, and Dornoch Firths (unlike the A9 main road nowadays). Another place the railway takes a much longer route is between Helmsdale and Wick; by road, it is about 35 miles, but by rail, it is 60 miles. The entire distance by road from Inverness to Wick is now about 102 miles following on from all the improvements of recent years, but the rail distance is 161.5 miles.

Continuing our July 1963 journey onwards from Helmsdale, instead of following the coast, the railway heads inland on tracks opened by the Sutherland and Caithness Railway in July 1874. This is to avoid the high ground of the Ord of Caithness, where even the A9 succumbs to a steep drop and hairpin bend at Berriedale. The route initially taken by the railway from Helmsdale is the sparsely inhabited Strath Ullie (Strath of Kildonan); it even included two 'platforms' where trains called by request at Salzcraggie (opened 1907) and Borrobol (opened about 1877) to serve isolated shooting lodges. The first crossing place, and where the first two photographs were taken, was Kildonan; here, time was spent waiting to pass the southbound 'Orcadian'. Something that always intrigued the author about this location was the '1868 Kildonan Gold Rush', plus another in 1896 after the railway had opened. Kildonan station also has a claim to fame in the modern world; according to Wikipedia, it is 'the least used station in the United Kingdom that has a full (i.e. not restricted) service'. The December 1966 issue of *Railway Magazine* states the cheery stationmaster at Kildonan was originally from Pakistan and wondered how he got on with life at such a remote place. Some 7.25 miles north from Kildonan was the next crossing place of Kinbrace, from where a connecting bus service used to run across the moors to Bettyhill on the north coast. (*Alan Maund*)

Above and opposite: The two major towns in the county of Caithnness are Wick, a port on the east coast at one time associated with the herring industry, and Thurso, the nearest port to the Orkneys. The 20 or so miles between Wick and Thurso are both relatively flat and fertile, and in the early 1860s, a railway was proposed between the two. The Caithness Railway was authorised in July 1866 with thoughts of an extension southwards to join the Sutherland Railway that had obtained its act in 1865. As authorised, it was a purely local concern and isolated from the national network, but funds were not forthcoming.

In the meantime, the Duke of Sutherland efforts saw the railway being extended to Helmsdale, and a new company was formed, the Sutherland and Caithness Railway. The S&CR proposed taking over the Caithness Railway and to follow the same route, both that already authorised between Wick and Thurso plus the southern extension. The new company received its act in July 1871, with the Highland Railway subscribing £50,000, and the Duke of Sutherland £60,000; the line opened on 28 July 1874. Georgemas Junction was created where the old Caithness Railway's 1866-authorised line from Wick to Thurso joined the Helmsdale southern extension. The name 'Georgemas' comes from an historic St George's Day fair held on nearby Sordale Hill (on which are several ancient cairns).

These are three more photographs taken by the late Alan Maund when he travelled over the Far North Line in July 1963; all are at Georgemas Junction where the connection from Thurso faces towards Wick (see also page 11). Firstly, in the view towards Wick taken from the now-demolished southbound platform, the train is beyond the end of the platform that curves back towards the Thurso branch. Secondly, the branch locomotive couples up to the arrival from Inverness and will take some of the rear coaches to Thurso; note the curved platform and the Inverness tracks on the right. Thirdly is a general view taken from the now-demolished station footbridge; the Thurso branch is to the right and the Inverness line to the centre. What appear to be long, wooden tables in the middle distance on the Inverness route at the commencement of the single track are, in fact, snow blowers; these funnel the prevailing wind at track level to sweep the snow clear. (*Alan Maund*)

Journey's end at the most northerly railway station on both the HR and BR's national system: Thurso. D5324 looks to have arrived with three coaches from Georgemas Junction in two final July 1963 photographs taken by Alan Maund. The HR came about following amalgamation of the Inverness and Aberdeen Junction and the Inverness and Perth Junction railways on 1 February 1865 (these two being themselves amalgamations of earlier companies); this combined undertaking was authorised to be known as the Highland Railway with headquarters at Inverness on 29 June 1865. At inception, the HR owned 242 route miles and operated over another 7.5 miles of Scottish North Eastern Railway track from Stanley Junction to Perth. The Dingwall and Skye Railway was merged on 2 August 1880 and then the Sutherland, Duke of Sutherland's, and Sutherland and Caithness railways joined the fold on 28 July 1884; these four lines added another 164.5 miles to the HR total. Its maximum extent, according to H. A. Vallance, was 506 miles and 31 chains; this was achieved in 1903 with the opening of the nominally independent Wick and Lybster Railway. (*Alan Maund*)

Following the Jacobite Rebellion of 1715, General Wade was sent to Scotland to create strategic roads at government expense that could be used for moving troops to put down any further rebellion; however, these military roads were largely unsuitable for trade in peacetime conditions. In 1803, the Government appointed Thomas Telford to survey new roads and carry out improvements to those already existing; in the next seventeen years, he built about 920 miles of road and some 1,200 bridges. Following this, stagecoaches were introduced and a partial trade revival resulted. Goods previously sent by sea could now often be sent much quicker by road, although it was the coming of the railway to the Highlands that most effectively solved the problem. These photographs with HR No. 103 are of the 'Scottish Rambler' rail tour on 21 April 1962. The location is Gollanfield, 9.5 miles east of Inverness, on the one-time Inverness and Nairn Railway that had opened in November 1855, making it the first railway to serve the Highland Capital. The bridge in the background carried an old military road to Fort George; Gollanfield had also been a junction station for the 1958-closed branch line to Fort George.

The first branch visited by the 'Scottish Rambler' tour on Easter Saturday 1962 was that from Alves (see page 2) to Burghead. Alves was on the main line from Inverness to Elgin and had been opened by the Inverness and Aberdeen Junction Railway in March 1858. Powers were obtained for the 5.5-mile-long Burghead branch on 17 May 1861, with the railway opening on 22 December 1862 to a station on the seafront. On 4 July 1890 powers were obtained to extend the branch two miles to Hopeman starting from just south of the original Burghead station. The extension opened on 10 October 1892 and a new Burghead station was built on it, the original becoming a goods depot. HR No. 103 is in the process of running around its train close to the original station by the sea shore, while the second shows a wagon on the south pier at the harbour (read description on page 12). The 1892-opened station at Burghead lost its passenger service in September 1931, freight continuing to the harbour until November 1966. Surprisingly, part of the branch from Alves still exists in a mothballed and overgrown state, but not that by the harbour.

In 1845, the Great North of Scotland Railway (GNSR) was formed to build a line from Aberdeen to Inverness via here at Elgin, and together with a proposed line from Aberdeen to Perth via Forfar (the later CR), it would have created a through (though rather circuitous) route to Inverness from the south. Yet a problem in the aftermath of the 'Railway Mania' was finance and the GNSR decided to limit itself to a line from Aberdeen to Keith, to where it opened in 1856. By August 1858, the Inverness and Aberdeen Junction Railway was open from Inverness through Elgin to Keith (via Mulben) and in conjunction with the GNSR provided a through over a 100-mile-long east–west route from Aberdeen to Inverness. However, the Morayshire Railway (closely associated with the I&AJR in its early days) was actually the first line at Elgin, opening from Lossiemouth on 10 August 1852. By 1858, the MR had reached Craigellachie (part-using I&AJR tracks), creating a north–south route from Lossiemouth; Elgin thus had railways to the four points of the compass. Further building and amalgamations occurred over the years, such that by the 1880s, there were three separate routes from Elgin to Keith: via Craigellachie (the MR amalgamating with the GNSR by an Act of 1881), via Mulben (HR from 1865), and via Cullen and the coast (GNSR open throughout by 1886). This view at the east end of Elgin station on Easter Saturday 1962 shows the 'Scottish Rambler' tour with HR No. 103 signalled to take the HR line to Keith, with the tracks forking left giving connection to the GNSR system that lost its passenger services later in the 1960s. The old HR line at Elgin sees a healthy passenger service today between Inverness and Aberdeen and is currently being upgraded as this book is being written. This excess fare ticket from Elgin to Perth is dated 9 November 1964.

Following the 'Railway Mania', finance was difficult to obtain, and the GNSR was forced to reconsider its original proposal for a through double-track line from Aberdeen to Inverness, settling for a single-track railway as far as Keith instead. Construction began in 1852 as far as Huntly, but the civil engineering works were built wide enough to take a second track sometime later. The railway opened to Huntly in September 1854 and then onwards to Keith in October 1856. At this time, the GNSR operated over about 54 miles of railway; ten years later, this had nearly quadrupled (although the majority was over leased or subsidiary lines), and just before the Grouping following the Railways Act of 1921, the company operated 333.5 route miles of track.

The joint BLS/SLS (Scottish Area) 'Scottish Rambler' rail tour that we have been following over the last few pages on Easter Saturday 1962 (ticket included) has now arrived at Insch and is taking on water. Rather appropriately, the locomotive used on former HR lines was HR No. 103, while at Keith there had been a change to the locomotive in this photograph, GNSR No. 49 *Gordon Highlander* that was used for the GNSR lines travelled over during the rest of that day.

The first meeting of promoters for the Banff, Macduff and Turriff Junction Railway took place on 23 October 1854; their plan was to build a nearly 30-mile-long line from the GNSR at Inveramsey northwards to fishing ports on the coast. The 18 miles to here at Turriff opened in September 1857, but passenger receipts were poor in the first year and even worse in the second. The directors were particularly incensed that the Post Office would not enter into the usual sort of agreement for mail to be carried at a fixed rate. The board held out hope that success would be achieved when the railway got through to Macduff, and the first sod of the Banff, Macduff and Turriff Extension Railway was cut on 27 July 1857. The company's bank (the City of Glasgow) collapsed in November 1857, but an injection of GNSR money kept things going and the line opened to a station called Banff and Macduff on 4 June 1860. It was a poor site. Banff was on the other side of the River Deveron and Macduff harbour was at the foot of a steep cliff. Also, Banff was served by an existing 1859-opened railway that became part of the GNSR fold in 1867. Despite the Turriff line offering substantial commissions to carriers, the bait proved unattractive and, in 1866, it was absorbed by the GNSR.

GNSR No. 49 *Gordon Highlander* stands at Turriff station on 21 April 1962 ready for its return to Inveramsey with the 'Scottish Rambler' tour. The entire branch had lost its passenger service on and from 1 October 1951, freight ceased north of Turriff from 1 August 1961, so at the time of this tour Turriff was the furthest point still open, and even it succumbed at the beginning of 1966. Both sides of this ticket from Kinloss to Forres dated Monday 28 July 1958 are included because of the pencil-written notes indicating it is for the first ever diesel trip from Aberdeen to Inverness.

The Caledonian Railway would eventually own, have vested in it, or a working arrangement for a chain of railways enabling a through journey from Carlisle to Aberdeen. Last in this northwards chain was the Aberdeen Railway authorised in July 1845. Early proposals envisaged the line running direct from Forfar via Brechin, but the bill as presented was for a junction along the Arbroath and Forfar Railway that saved on new construction (the A&FR had been built to a gauge of 5 feet 6 inches so gauge-conversion was also required). It resulted in Brechin being served by a connecting branch from Bridge of Dun on the main line; this opened on 1 February 1848 and before the through route to Aberdeen was finished. Both views are at Brechin during a visit of the 'Scottish Rambler' tour on Easter Sunday 1962 (see also page 7). Passenger services had ceased in August 1952 (freight continuing until 1981) but everything still appears neat and tidy; even the station clock looks to be showing the correct time as the tour was at Brechin at 10.30 a.m. These views can still be appreciated today as the station is home to the heritage Caledonian Railway (Brechin) Ltd.

Edzell is a village about 6 miles north of Brechin, yet despite the fact its population was fewer than 1,000 in the 1890s, Royal Assent was given to the Brechin and Edzell District Railway in August 1890. As originally authorised, the line was to have its own terminus in Brechin, but other railway building in the area (the Forfar and Brechin Railway) forced the B&EDR to go back to Parliament in 1893 for a change of route plus authority to use the station at Brechin seen in the previous commentary. The line opened for goods on 1 June 1896 and to passengers one week later. By February 1919, there were three or four passenger services each way with one extra on Saturdays, but nothing on Sundays; the CR worked the line for 50 per cent of the receipts. The branch closed to passengers in 1931, but was reopened for an experimental period in the summer of 1938 that was deemed unsuccessful. The 1962 'Scottish Rambler' is seen at Edzell on Easter Sunday with D8028 as motive power. Freight finally came to an end in September 1964 and, with it, total closure at Edzell.

Above and opposite: The main line to Aberdeen from the south took an inland route and left 37 miles of coast from Arbroath to Stonehaven without a railway, except the branch from Dubton to Montrose. Failing to arouse the interest of larger companies, local people decided to promote a line themselves and the Montrose and Bervie Railway was floated in 1860. After two years, the promoters were on the point of giving up when they found themselves caught up in railway politics. The GNSR came up with a plan to get hold of the M&BR and extend it north along the coast to Stonehaven, where it would join the existing line to Aberdeen, while to the south, their idea was to link up with the line from Dundee to Arbroath that had opened in the 1830s. With running powers exercised from Dundee to Arbroath and from Stonehaven to Aberdeen, the GNSR would have had the entire coast from the Tay to the Dee in its grasp. The result was the GNSR poured money into the coffers of the M&BR; however, the dream was short-lived and the bill concerned was thrown out. The M&BR reverted back to their original plan and work started, the idea being to have it all finished by the summer of 1865; the line actually opened in the November.

In 1872, the M&BR again found itself as a pawn. The North British Railway operated a service from Edinburgh to Aberdeen that included ferries over the Forth and Tay as well as working over the lines of other companies. The NBR's long-term plan was to remedy these with bridges and new railways to join with the CR at Kinnaber. To some, it was thought that when the NBR absorbed the M&BR in 1881, it might revive plans of an extension to Stonehaven, but this was not to be.

All three photographs were taken on 22 May 1962 and show the 'Scottish Rambler' hauled by D8028 (and also the tour ticket). Firstly, the original terminus (to the right) at Montrose opened by the Aberdeen Railway in 1848 (CR from 1866) on the line from Dubton; this station had closed to passengers in April 1934. Secondly, Inverbervie (renamed from Bervie in 1926) is where the old turntable pit is prominent and also defences from the Second World War. Finally, Johnshaven station is seen on the return to Montrose. Passenger services over the branch ceased on and from 1 October 1951, although freight continued until May 1966.

Above and opposite: Quarries on high ground near Carmyllie (about 6 miles west of Arbroath) became important for producing roofing slate and later paving stones. Transport to Arbroath for onwards coastal shipping was first by horse and cart. Then, a mineral branch was built as a private undertaking from Elliot Junction (south-west of Arbroath) to the quarries around Carmyllie by Lord Panmure with an opening around January 1855. By 1870, quarry output was at its peak, employing some 300 people, but production declined after 1900 and the quarries closed before the First World War. New management restarted production in 1922, on a much smaller scale; sixteen were employed in 1938, and only a few remained when the quarries closed in 1953.

The question of passenger trains was raised over the years and was made possible by the Light Railways Act of 1896 with a service starting on 1 February 1900; it was the first in Scotland to be so operated, by then under joint CR and NBR ownership (since 1880). The passenger service was suspended for a time during the First World War and by February 1919 consisted of two trains daily each way except Sundays; this service ceased for good on 2 December 1929.

When the line was built, mention was made of the 'extensive agricultural district'; it was this that kept the line alive in later years, especially potatoes. The branch was steep with a maximum grade of 1 in 36 and the quarries themselves were some 600 feet above sea level. It was also lightly laid, hence the use of Ivatt Class 2 2-6-0s Nos 46463 and 46464 on the Easter Sunday 1962 'Scottish Rambler'. The first photograph shows some of the 'extensive agricultural district', while the second is at Carmyllie itself (although the station was actually in the village of Redford). The final photograph is approaching Elliot Junction on the return with the Elliot Water on the right; the train has just passed through a cutting known locally as 'The Gullet' that is now a nature walk. The branch closed in May 1965 although a section was kept by the main line that connected to the Metal Box factory until 1984.

Forfar eventually developed into a railway crossroads, the first line to arrive being the Arbroath and Forfar Railway. Built to a gauge of 5 feet 6 inches, this was initially horse-operated and the first train arrived at the original Forfar Playfield station on 4 December 1838. The first locomotive arrival was at the beginning of January 1839. The line was converted to standard-gauge in 1847, and Greenwich Time was adopted in 1848 instead of local time. Gauge-conversion had become essential as there were a mass of railway authorisations in the mid-1840s that would link together and form a through standard-gauge route from Carlisle to Aberdeen.

Due to the difficulty crossing the Tay, it became obvious Perth was going to become an important railway centre, and the Scottish Midland Junction Railway (CR from 1866) opened from Perth to the station in this photograph at Forfar in 1848. The original station then closed to passengers but continued with freight, and, by 1850, the link onwards to Aberdeen (unbroken from London) was complete. In 1870, a line was opened southwards to Dundee, and, in 1895, a direct route to Brechin. By the 1890s, the line to Forfar from Perth had been upgraded and became something of a racing ground. The first ever 60-mph start-to-stop run published in *Bradshaw* was the 32.5 miles from Forfar to Perth with the up West Coast Postal that was run in thirty-two minutes. This view is taken at the east end of Forfar Station on Easter Monday, 23 April 1962, with No. 54465 in charge of the 'Scottish Rambler'. The last passenger trains called at Forfar on Sunday, 3 September 1967, after which freight only carried on from the Perth direction until 1982.

A few pages earlier, it was described how in the 1840s Brechin was left off the main line (CR from 1866) to Aberdeen from the south. Thoughts of the original route via Brechin were revived in the 1880s, and the Forfar and Brechin Railway received its act in August 1890. Although conceived as a through route, it joined the line from Perth to the west of Forfar, thus not serving the latter. Also, the existing terminal station at Brechin faced the centre of the town and could not be converted to a through station. There were further problems with the Edzell branch seen earlier that was authorised concurrently with the F&BR; the routes of the two lines had not been coordinated at Brechin and the Edzell company had to go back to Parliament for a further act. The result was the F&BR sold out to the CR before completion and the line opened in 1895. It never achieved its aim as a trunk route because any through services would have required reversals at both Forfar and Brechin; instead, it settled down to life as a rural branch. In February 1919, there were just three passenger trains each way on weekdays only. This photograph is taken at Careston on 23 April 1962 with No. 54465 running around the 'Scottish Rambler' tour; this locomotive was the last 'Caley Bogie' in working condition (according to the SLS house magazine) and had been specially brought north from Motherwell for the tour. Passenger services throughout ceased on and from 4 August 1952 and the track behind the locomotive onwards to Brechin had been removed following closure to freight in March 1958. Careston continued with freight until September 1964 when it was cut back to Justinhaugh; the final section back to the main line west of Forfar closed in September 1967.

Due to its natural geography, Perth became an important railway centre from the mid-1840s, all railways north and east of here on their way to Glasgow and Edinburgh having to pass through the city until opening of the Tay Bridge. As early as 1850, four separate lines converged at Perth: the Scottish Central from Stirling and the south-west; the Edinburgh and Northern from the south-east including a ferry crossing of the Forth; the Dundee, Perth and Aberdeen Junction from the east; and the Scottish Midland Junction from the north. Later, subsequent construction would see other railways entering the city, and, in 1863, the Perth General Station Joint Committee was set up.

Perth occupied a special place in Queen Victoria's journeys to and from Balmoral. On the northbound journey, her entire entourage took breakfast at the adjoining station hotel. There was also considerable marshalling of long and heavy trains. Expresses from the HR had separate sections for the West Coast, Midland, and East Coast routes. Very long platforms over 1,400 feet in length were provided and had scissor crossings in the middle, enabling the combining of trains or allowing two trains to be worked from one platform, although Dundee traffic was not and still is not handled under the main roof.

The Easter Monday 1962 'Scottish Rambler' tour catches the morning sun at the north end of Perth station where it stands ready for an 8.30 a.m. start. It is double-headed with CR 4-4-0 No. 54465 and CR 0-6-0T No. 56347, which would together take this five-coach special the 5 miles to Strathord and the next commentary (see also page 16).

The first branch line visited by the 'Scottish Rambler' rail tour after departure from Perth in the previous commentary on Easter Monday 23 April 1962 was the Bankfoot Light Railway (ticket included). A Light Railway Order for this 3-mile-long branch was obtained on 19 November 1898. It diverged from the main CR line to Aberdeen 5 miles north of Perth at Strathord (originally Dunkeld Road). A further Light Railway Order was granted in 1903 and the BLR opened on 5 March 1906. The branch was worked by the CR before being acquired by them in 1913. By February 1919, the passenger service was four return workings from Bankfoot to Strathord with one extra on Saturdays but nothing on Sundays. The branch passenger service ceased on and from 13 April 1931, plus Strathord station on the main line closed at the same time. No. 56347 is seen at Bankfoot station that comprised a single platform with a wooden building and to its side was the goods shed plus a number of sidings. Freight traffic continued until total closure of the branch in September 1964.

The author has found something of a mystery here. A number of references state both Nos 56347 and 54465 that hauled the special from Perth were also both used on the Bankfoot branch. I only travelled on the Good Friday 1962 'Scottish Rambler' and so did not visit Bankfoot on this day, but, looking at the ciné film taken by my father plus also the stills and ciné taken by a friend who accompanied him, there is no evidence whatsoever of No. 54465 being at Bankfoot. Perhaps there is someone who can remember what happened nearly sixty years ago and solve this Bankfoot mystery.

The Newburgh and North Fife Railway received assent in August 1897 for a 13.25-mile line along the south bank of the Tay, but work did not start until June 1906 and further visits to Parliament were required. The N&NFR ran from St Fort to Glenburnie Junction near Newburgh; the eastern end was thought ripe for residential development due to Dundee's proximity. The single-track line opened in January 1909 and engineering was on the prodigious scale. There were deep cuttings, substantial bridges, the signalling system was called 'the most perfect and up-to-date', and it was able to carry the heaviest NBR stock. The NBR undertook to work the line for 50 per cent of receipts, guarantee a 4 per cent dividend, and give a traffic guarantee. Yet things did not work out as hoped; there was much legal toing and froing, and the line ended up as a rural backwater. Passenger services ceased in February 1951 with total closure in October 1964. The 'Scottish Rambler' tour is seen on Easter Sunday 1962 with 'J39' No. 64786 at Kilmany and then running around at Lindores; the line onwards to Glenburnie Junction having been closed in April 1960.

With dieselisation of the East Coast Main Line well underway by the early 1960s, there became less and less work for Gresley's famous streamlined 'A4s'. The last scheduled steam-hauled expresses at London King's Cross had been in June 1963; one year later, all remaining 'A4s' in service bar one had been transferred to Scotland (No. 60001 lasted at Gateshead until October 1964). A trial had been carried out with No. 60027 between Glasgow and Aberdeen in February 1962 and deemed a success. The surviving 'A4s' were used on the tightly timed three-hour expresses between Glasgow and Aberdeen plus other duties such as the West Coast Postal from Aberdeen to Perth or Carstairs. Apparently, the Aberdeen and Perth drivers took to their new steeds, but those at Glasgow were, in the main, hostile. A threat to re-diagram duties in favour of Perth and Aberdeen silenced the problem and the 'A4s' settled down to several years of good work on the route until all had been withdrawn by September 1966. Both views are at Gleneagles of No. 60006 *Sir Ralph Wedgewood* arriving and departing with a southbound express on 4 June 1965 (see also page 12); No. 60006 would be withdrawn three months later. (*Alan Maund*)

Ceremonial breaking of ground for the Fife and Kinross Railway took place here at Auchtermuchty on 14 January 1856, a 14-mile line from Ladybank to Kinross. There had been considerable opposition in Parliament, but once construction started, things moved quickly. It was open through Auchtermuchty within eighteen months, all the way to Kinross by August 1858, but by 1862, the line was in the hands of the NBR. In February 1919, passenger services consisted of four trains each way (weekdays only) between Ladybank and Kinross Junction, one of which worked to and from Stirling via Alloa and the Devon Valley. Passenger services ceased on 5 June 1950 and the line east of Auchtermuchty closed totally in 1957. NBR No. 256 *Glen Douglas* is seen east of the station by Auchtermuchty signal box with the 'Scottish Rambler No. 2' rail tour on 13 April 1963 and then at the station itself. On the way back, the tour was delayed when three sheep found themselves trapped between fences on either side of the track and, despite the train crew proceeding cautiously, one of them was run over. Auchtermuchty lost its freight service in 1964.

2nd - Class
STEPHENSON LOCOMOTIVE SOCIETY
and
BRANCH LINE SOCIETY
13th April 1963.
Edinburgh (Waverley) to
EDINBURGH (WAVERLEY)
via SouthQueensferry KinglassieDollar & Alva
For conditions see over (H
0048

At a young age, the author developed a keen interest in railway timetables and would read through them looking for things out of the ordinary. An example that ticked more than one box was the line from Kinross Junction to Alloa; it had a very sparse passenger service plus some strange names to go with it. The line is the Devon Valley Railway, which to young Michael seemed a particularly odd name to find in Scotland, and then there were some seemingly peculiar station names such as Dollar and here at Rumbling Bridge. I did manage just a single journey over the line, and this is it, the 'Scottish Rambler No. 2' rail tour on Easter Saturday 1963 with NBR No. 256 *Glen Douglas* (ticket included).

The Devon Valley Railway provided the missing link in a through secondary route between the Forth and the Tay. When completed in 1871, it was worked by the NBR (absorbed in 1875) and gave the company a mostly single-track, diagonal route across Fife, Kinross, and Clackmannan from Ladybank to Alloa. After opening of the first Tay Bridge in 1878, through carriages were run from Edinburgh and Glasgow to Dundee and Aberdeen by this route. Following opening of the Forth Bridge in 1890, the NBR had two routes: 'The Historic Route' via the newly built Forth Bridge and 'The Picturesque Route' via the Devon Valley.

The rather isolated station at Rumbling Bridge had a passing loop and took its name from the nearby bridge over the Devon; here, the river pours over a series of falls and, after heavy rain, it is said the river 'rumbles' through its confined rocky channel. A service of six or seven weekday trains was provided between Alloa and Kinross for many years, but the line suffered in post-Second World War economies; by 1960, there were only two through services. By the beginning of 1964, there was just a single return diesel through service each way daily (except Sundays) from Stirling via Alloa, the Devon Valley, and Kinross Junction to Perth; the line through Rumbling Bridge was totally closed on 15 June 1964.

The earliest form of railway in Clackmannanshire was the horse-operated single track Alloa Waggonway; this dated from the 1760s and delivered coal from north of Alloa to Alloa Harbour. The coming of 'proper' railways reduced the importance of the Waggonway that here ran along the top of the cutting on the right and behind of both photographs, where there used to be a passing loop; today, this is part of a footpath and cycleway. The 'Scottish Rambler No. 2' rail tour on 13 April 1963 has arrived close to Alloa East signal box from Rumbling Bridge in the previous commentary. A change of motive power was required and NBR No. 256 would be replaced by Dunfermline-allocated 'J36' No. 65323, seen in the second photograph (see also the introductory photograph on page 2). Although the line from Kinross to Alloa that the *Glen Douglas* has just travelled over closed as a through route in 1964, the lower portion to here remained open serving the coal mine at Dollar until 1973.

It is near-impossible to remember who took particular photographs approaching sixty years ago—was it my father or was it me? This is one of the few cases where the evidence can be seen. Around the early 1960s, generally speaking, I took the monochrome photos and my father the colour slides. To the left in the colour photograph, the young lad in short trousers is me, and if you look very closely, you can see the Halina camera around my neck that will have been used to take this black-and-white photograph; my father was using a Super Baldina camera with Kodachrome II colour film. On 22 July 1861, the Alva Railway was authorised to connect the weaving towns of Alva and Menstrie with the Stirling to Dunfermline route at Cambus, the line opening on 3 June 1863. From Alva to Alloa by rail is very indirect, with the passenger service succumbing on and from 1 November 1954. Both photographs show No. 65323 at Alva ready for its return to Alloa hauling the 'Scottish Rambler No. 2' tour on Easter Saturday 1963. Freight continued to Alva until the beginning of March 1964.

A rail tour the author recalls as being something of a disaster with the weather, the locomotives, and the timekeeping was the 'Scottish Rambler No. 5' tour on Easter Saturday, 9 April 1966 (ticket included). The tour started from Glasgow Buchanan Street with 'V2' No. 60919, which had to be taken off at Falkirk Grahamston with what was believed to be valve gear problems. It is seen in the monochrome photograph having retired to a siding and was replaced by D6115 that took the tour onwards. At Dunfermline Lower in the second photograph is the steam replacement, 'B1' No. 61407, which continued with the tour to Dundee. A trip was also attempted along the Inverbervie branch but had to be abandoned, and I believe we eventually got back to Glasgow Buchanan Street well after midnight. Not content with this ignominy, No. 60919 disgraced itself again some three months later on 3 July 1966. It had been specially sent hundreds of miles from its home depot at Dundee to the south of England for a rail tour we filmed—'The Green Arrow'—but it failed again and substitute locomotives had to be used.

For years, the standard freight locomotive on many of the railways of Britain was the humble 0-6-0, and the locomotive in this photograph represents the final development of its type on the NBR: the 'J37'. They were a superheated development of the earlier 'J35' and also had larger cylinders. Construction started in 1914 with production ramped up after the First World War, the orders being shared between the NBR's own works at Cowlairs and the North British Locomotive Company. They were initially allocated to long-distance goods and mineral services on the NBR's main lines and proved most useful with the extra wartime loads. In total, 104 locomotives were built and all survived into Nationalisation. Withdrawals started slowly in 1959; thirteen still remained in service in June 1966, operating short-distance goods and coal trains in the Lowlands and Fife, with the last examples surviving into 1967, the final year of BR Scottish-allocated steam. This photograph of a spruced-up No. 64618 was taken at Thornton Junction; it was about to work the 'Scottish Rambler No. 2' rail tour to Leslie on Easter Saturday 1963. No. 64618 was withdrawn from Thornton Junction shed in the autumn of 1966.

The most southerly point in Fife is North Queensferry, which is also the narrowest place to cross the Firth of Forth; as a result, it has always been a natural place to access the far side. The northern end of the Forth Rail Bridge is also at North Queensferry, but a major problem for the railway is the tracks are 150 feet above the water. As a result, there are steep grades on both the southern (1 in 100) and northern (1 in 70) approaches. Two commentaries earlier, I related how behind time the rail tour on 9 April 1966 we travelled on was getting back to Glasgow; part of this lateness was attributable to the gradient of 1 in 70 between Inverkeithing and here at North Queensferry. The Inverness to York car-sleeper had stalled on the grade and our tour locomotive, the famous and now-preserved No. 60532 *Blue Peter*, was borrowed to help the stalled train up the 1 in 70.

North Queensferry station is seen in about 1961 with a southbound service arriving and will have just climbed up the grade from Inverkeithing. The locomotive is 'B1' No. 61245 *Murray of Elibank*, named after a director of the LNER. (*Alan Maund*)

Two more photographs from the Alan Maund archive, both taken at Bathgate and believed to date from about 1961. In the background of the first is the Edinburgh Road and the second is taken close to Bathgate Central signal box. Both locomotives are NBR 'J36s', Nos 65277 and 65282, an exceptionally long-lived class. They were introduced in 1888, and 168 had been built when production ceased in 1900. Used all over the NBR system, they initially hauled long-distance goods services. During the First World War, twenty-five were loaned to the Government and saw use in France. At the Grouping in 1923, Bathgate engine shed had an allocation of twenty-three 'J36s'. As the years went by, the class saw more use on local mineral traffic and also branch line passenger services, with their light weight allowing them to work almost anywhere. Although the first withdrawal was in 1926 (following an accident), 123 survived to Nationalisation, and six were still at work in 1966. The final two were withdrawn in June 1967 and outlasted all other BR Scottish-allocated steam. (*Alan Maund*)

Above and opposite: The author and his father only ever visited the old NBR engine shed at St Margarets, Edinburgh, the once, on Saturday, 5 October 1963, when all three photographs were taken. The occasion was the RCTS 'Duchess Commemorative' rail tour from Crewe to Edinburgh Princes Street and back in a day. We left home in Worcestershire before 6 a.m. and did not get back until about midnight. Arrival at Edinburgh was at 2.10 p.m. and departure back to Crewe at 3.48 p.m., but in that time, a visit was made to this shed. It was located south of the East Coast Main Line, to the east of Edinburgh Waverley station, and was a very cramped location. It has been described as a dark smoky hole, and I do not imagine residents of the housing visible close by thought much to it either.

In the first photograph, 'A1' No. 60151 *Midlothian* had actually been built by the Nationalised BR in 1948 at Darlington, although it was to an LNER design. With dieselisation of the express passenger services, No. 60151 was transferred to Tweedmouth in 1962 and often used on goods work. 'V2' No. 60929 was allocated to York at this time and is adjacent to the ECML tracks. The author's interest was rather taken by 'N15' No. 69138; it had been withdrawn a year previously and was rusting away in a quiet corner. Our friend Eric Parker listed fifty-three locomotives on shed this day at St Margarets in his diaries.

The journey back to Crewe proved quite spectacular; the 32.2 miles from Tebay to Lancaster (pass to pass) were run in twenty-four minutes and three seconds, with No. 46251 *City of Nottingham* at an average speed above 80 mph—believed to be an all-time record for steam.

THE DUCHESS COMMEMORATIVE RAILTOUR

SATURDAY, 5th OCTOBER, 1963

This tour has been arranged by the Railtour Sub-Committee (Messrs. W. H. Ashcroft, J. D. Farquhar, and N. A. Machell) of the Lancashire and North West Branch of the Society, to give members and their friends what may prove to be a last opportunity to travel over Shap and Beattock behind a locomotive of the ex-L.M.S. "Coronation" class on express passenger timings. The suggestion for such a tour first came from a member who, on hearing that the class might be barred from operating over the newly electrified line south of Crewe, felt that a special should be arranged on the last day before the ban became effective. The matter was still under active consideration when events caught up with us somewhat and information was received that the "Lizzies", as they are known to railwaymen, were to be withdrawn from service at the end of 1963. On the strength of this information, the Branch Committee decided that a far more interesting run would be northwards from Crewe, and the threat of the "Beeching Axe" over Princes St. Station determined our ultimate destination for us. Negotiations were immediately commenced with the London Midland Region and the result is our journey today. The ready co-operation of the railway authorities in agreeing to our every request has considerably eased the work of organising this tour and our appreciation of this is acknowledged.

To meet the occasion it was decided that something rather more substantial than the usual railtour itinerary was called for, and the help of all those who assisted in bringing this booklet to fruition is also acknowledged.

At the time of going to press the expected make up of the train is of eleven ex-L.M.S. coaches including cafeteria car facilities, and our locomotive for the whole round trip 46256 *Sir William A. Stanier, F.R.S.* This locomotive, whilst not wholly of the original pattern, was chosen for three reasons, these being (i) the name it carries, (ii) it was the last Pacific built by the L.M.S., and (iii) it is in red livery.

The Branch Committee hope that you will have an enjoyable day.

(26665)
British Railways Board (M)
Railway Correspondence & Travel ...
X68   5th October, 196...
The "Duchess" Commemorative Rail-Tour
Crewe/Warrington B.Q./Preston/Carlisle
to Edinburgh (Princes Street) and Return
via the West Coast Main Line and the
Carstairs avoiding line, with a locomotive
of the ex-L.M.S. "Princess Coronation"
class.
SECOND CLASS   For conditions see over

Despite the above taken from the tour's souvenir booklet (my child ticket also included), No. 46256 *Sir William A. Stanier, F.R.S.* developed a defect with its front bogie a week previous to the tour. It was replaced on the day with No. 46251 *City of Nottingham.*

Above, below and next page: The RCTS-organised 'Scottish Lowlander' on 26 September 1964 was said to be one of the most epic of all time in terms of locomotive performance. It was the last ever pre-preservation working of a 'Coronation Pacific' and, rather appropriately, the stationmaster at Crewe saw us off on time in his top hat; the tour was nearly 550 miles long. There was a locomotive change at Carlisle from No. 46256 *Sir William A. Stanier, F.R.S.* to 'A4' No. 60007 *Sir Nigel Gresley*, but things did not go according to plan. Two incidents happened at Carlisle that seem to have been related: firstly, the special was announced as being a service train for Glasgow and 'normal' passengers joined our train; and secondly, on departure, the special was signalled for the CR route to Glasgow rather than the NBR 'Waverley Route' to Edinburgh it should have taken. Eric Parker recorded us six minutes late away from Carlisle; there was also the extra delay by being signalled on the wrong route and having to reverse. Yet these incidents set the stage for a dramatic time recovery climbing the grades up to Whitrope Summit on the way to Hawick. According to the *Railway Observer*, an estimated drawbar horsepower in the range of 2,000–2,100 at about 36 mph was maintained for fifteen minutes, thought to be the highest ever sustained in this speed range for the class, with the 'A4s' being designed as high-speed locomotives.

This put the special back on schedule, but another problem then raised its head as a consequence. To develop such high power requires a lot of coal to be burnt and the authorities were concerned that No. 60007 might not have enough left to complete its journey all the way back to Carlisle. There was a reserve 'A4', No. 60009 *Union of South Africa*, and its services were now called upon. At Niddrie West Junction, Edinburgh, the locomotives were changed over; the junction signal box was partly visible to the right of No. 60009's tender. The front cover of the tour itinerary is also included.

THE
RAILWAY CORRESPONDENCE AND TRAVEL SOCIETY

60004 *William Whitelaw* near New Cumnock on 30th June, 1963
(From a photograph by R. A. Lissenden)

ITINERARY OF THE
SCOTTISH LOWLANDER

Saturday, 26th September, 1964

Tour organised by the Lancashire and North West Branch

The fertile and level area of Berwickshire known as the Merse extends about 20 miles along the north bank of the Tweed and is about 10 miles in breadth; it is centred on the one-time county town of Duns (until local government changes in the 1970s). The first railway reached Duns from a junction with (what is now) the East Coast Main Line at Reston. The branch opened in August 1849, had been built by the NBR, and was 8.5 miles long with double track. In 1862, the Berwickshire Railway was formed with the purpose of extending the line 21 miles westwards from Duns to Ravenswood Junction on the 'Waverley Route' near to St Boswells; the NBR subscribed £50,000 to its construction costs. The first sod was cut at Greenlaw (then the county town of Berwickshire) on 14 October 1862, and the complete route was open by the beginning of October 1865. Although single track, enough land was taken for possible double track later, despite the double track from Duns to Reston having already been converted to single.

By February 1919, there was a service of four or five passenger trains daily each way on weekdays from Duns to both Reston and St Boswells, including two return workings over the 42 miles from Berwick to St Boswells. During the August 1948 floods, all services were suspended between Duns and Greenlaw as the track had been washed away; they were never restored. Passenger services continued to Duns from Reston until that ceased on 10 September 1951, with freight continuing until November 1966. This photograph shows the 'Scottish Rambler No. 2' rail tour on 14 April 1963 hauled by 'B1' No. 61324 in the process of running around at Duns in a view looking towards the west; the tour ticket is also included.

The only place included in the main body of this book that is not in Scotland: Wooler in Northumberland. In the previous commentary, we were on the north side of the River Tweed at Duns, from where the 'Scottish Rambler No. 2' rail tour travelled to Tweedmouth for a change of motive power to the locomotive in this photograph. Tweedmouth-allocated lightweight Ivatt Class 2 2-6-0 No. 46474 took over (despite a respected reference saying it was 'B1' No. 61324) for the run along the south side of the Tweed to Coldstream (Cornhill previous to 1873), where the station was in England but the town in Scotland.

In 1881, the North Eastern Railway put plans before Parliament for a 36-mile line from Alnwick to Coldstream via Wooler, which was open throughout by September 1887. The line was single and Wooler was the only station with two separate platforms. Following the development of road transport after the First World War, the line found it could not hold its own against competing bus services and the passenger service ceased on 22 September 1930; Wooler only had a passenger service for forty-three years. Freight continued along the full length of the railway until the August 1948 floods cut the line. From then on, it was operated as two separate branches—southwards from Coldstream to Wooler, and northwards from Alnwick to Ilderton; the line was never repaired between Wooler and Ilderton. Freight continued to Wooler from Coldstream until March 1965. No. 46474 is seen at Wooler on Easter Sunday, 14 April 1963, having just run around its train. After arrival back at Coldstream, 'B1' No. 61324 took charge again, the 'B1' being too heavy for the Wooler branch.

The final change of motive power with the 'Scottish Rambler No. 2' tour on Easter Sunday, 14 April 1963, was at Hawick. The time was about 6.45 p.m.; it had started to rain and it was getting dark. 'B1' No. 61342 handed over at Hawick to 'A3' No. 60041 *Salmon Trout* and lamps are being attached, the strange name being the racehorse that won the 1924 St Ledger.

Gresley's first class of 4-6-2 'Pacifics' were the 'A1s', big and imposing locomotives when the first member of the class appeared in 1922. Following the Grouping, they became the standard express passenger locomotive for the newly formed London and North Eastern Railway (LNER). Yet they suffered embarrassment when comparative tests were run in 1925 against the GWR 'Castle' class, a significantly smaller 4-6-0 locomotive. Following this ignominy, improvements were made, such as altering the valve gear in accordance with GWR practice, increasing the boiler pressure, and increasing the steam temperature. New-build locomotives with the improvements were classed as 'A3s' and nicknamed 'Super Pacifics', the older 'A1s' being brought up to the new standard. Until the coming of the streamlined 'A4's in 1935, they hauled the premier expresses on the LNER, including non-stop runs between London and Edinburgh.

Improvements were still being carried out to the 'A3s' until very late in the day and two can be seen on No. 60041: firstly, the double chimney fitted in July 1959; and secondly, the trough-type smoke deflectors that had only been fitted three months previous to this photograph. These were attached during a general repair at Doncaster works that also included a change of boiler, which probably explains why No. 60041 was the last but one 'A3' to remain in service, being withdrawn at the beginning of December 1965 from St Margarets shed, Edinburgh.

The NBR's 'Waverley Route' ran 98.25 miles from Edinburgh to Carlisle via Galashiels and Hawick; it was open throughout by 1862, the CR route via Beattock being about a couple of miles further. This new interloper at Carlisle was not welcomed by the West Coast companies who made a secret agreement to ensure traffic went via the CR and not the NBR. This proved so effective that even locomotive parts ordered by the NBR from the Midlands went from Carlisle to Edinburgh over CR metals. Things changed with the opening of the Midland Railway's Settle to Carlisle line that provided another route to London and the south from Carlisle (as it also did for the G&SWR); a through service from Edinburgh to London St Pancras started in 1876. Dr Beeching's dislike of duplicate routes meant it came under scrutiny following his famous 1963 report and the last trains ran in January 1969. The first photograph is near Shankend as A4 No. 60031 *Golden Plover* heads an enthusiasts' special to Carlisle on 18 April 1965. The second shows the 'Scottish Lowlander' close to Whitrope Siding with No. 60007 *Sir Nigel Gresley* on 26 September 1964.